OUR LADY
OF CHARITY

T0061987

"*¡Excelente!* In this brilliant primer on Our Lady of Charity of el Cobre, Maria Morera Johnson skillfully captures a Marian devotion that unites all Cubans around the globe—their love for a familiar Mother who leads all to Jesus. Weaving memoir, history, and facts, Johnson's personal and often humorous anecdotes are insightfully sincere and disarmingly tender. Johnson may be my fellow exile, fellow immigrant, fellow cubana, fellow pilgrim, and thanks to our common name, a tocaya to boot! But nothing connects us more as sisters than our profound affection for our *Cachita,* our *virgencita—Nuestra Señora de la Caridad,* patron of Cuba, the island of our birth."

María Ruiz Scaperlanda
Catholic author, blogger, and journalist

"Maria Morera Johnson's deep cultural and familial devotion as a Cuban American to Our Lady of Charity, *la virgencita,* instantly draws the reader in and makes the reader feel like part of the family—the Holy Family! This book is a must-read for anyone wishing to understand the deep relationship many cultures have with Our Lady and for those longing to know her as their own Mother."

Noelle Garcia
Catholic speaker and recording artist

"A gifted storyteller, Maria Morera Johnson takes the reader on a life-transforming adventure through the history of a country torn apart, sharing the traditions and a powerful devotion that sustained and nurtured an oppressed people. In the midst of seeming chaos, an intense devotion to Our Lady of Charity shines forth as a beacon of hope. Johnson's deep love of Mary, her passion for sharing her devotion to Our Lady of El Cobre, and her undying love of her Catholic faith embrace and welcome the reader, making one feel like a beloved member of a beautiful Catholic-Cuban family. In a time when love has been relegated to just one of many emotions, Johnson brings this virtue to the forefront—its rightful place."

Kelly M. Wahlquist
Founder of WINE: Women In the New Evangelization

"Fueled by compelling historical and cultural context, *Our Lady of Charity* delivers a profound message of faith and consolation. Join Maria Morera Johnson as she invites you to better know Jesus Christ through Mary, a constant source of deliverance and love. This book is the perfect life preserver for the storms that challenge your daily journey!"

Lisa M. Hendey
Founder of *CatholicMom.com*

OUR LADY OF CHARITY

HOW A *Cuban* DEVOTION TO *Mary* HELPED ME *Grow* IN *Faith* AND *Love*

MARIA MORERA JOHNSON

Author of *My Badass Book of Saints*

AVE MARIA PRESS AVE Notre Dame, Indiana

© 2019 by Maria Morera Johnson

Founded in 1865, Ave Maria Press is a ministry of the United States Province of Holy Cross.

www.avemariapress.com

Paperback: ISBN-13 978-1-59471-901-1

E-book: ISBN-13 978-1-59471-902-8

Cover images © Lava4images, georgeclerk, and ttinu/Adobestock.

Our Lady of Charity art by Verde y Azul, www.etsy.com/shop/ArtTepuy.

Cover and text design by Katherine Robinson.

Printed and bound in the United States of America.

Library of Congress Cataloging-in-Publication Data is available.

For my children and grandchildren,
Que la virgen los acompañe.

CONTENTS

*J*NTRODUCTION

Sometimes I make my mother crazy. It's good-na-tured—mostly just a little teasing about outrageous things I have no intention of actually doing. I say something silly; she feigns outrage. We both laugh. Then she squints her eyes at me, "You're not going to do that, right?"

I never do. Except that one time I asked Pope Francis for a selfie.

• • •

In the fall of 2015, I was trying to figure out how I would join some friends in Philadelphia, Pennsylvania, for Pope Francis's visit to the United States for the World Meeting of Families when my sister called to ask if instead I would go to Cuba to see the pope with our mother.

Well. Yes.

I was being given the extraordinary opportunity to visit Cuba during Pope Francis's apostolic visit, but it wasn't as easy as just wanting to go.

I left Cuba in 1965, and I had never been back. I have family in Cuba. I had, for decades, a deep yearning to someday return to the land where I was born and to see with my own eyes the sights my parents had described with loving detail. It was one of those dreams we have and then safely store away. I had placed my dream of returning to Cuba on a shelf, stacked neatly next to other dreams such as writing a book or retiring to a waterfront home. One day, when we finished raising the children. When we have the money. When we retire.

I think the Blessed Mother had her own ideas about the timing.

Jesus, the Blessed Mother, and Me

Ever since I made my total consecration to Jesus through Mary, I'd been making every effort to turn over my fears and desires to Mary. I knew this consecration was a prayerful way to devote myself more fully to Jesus. I was confident that, through Mary's intercession and grace, whatever was on my heart would be resolved, whether it was a fear, a deep desire of my heart, or this yearning to someday visit Cuba.

I'm sure my heavenly mother, under the title of Our Lady of Charity of El Cobre, wanted me to return to Cuba, too. So in late 2015, I found myself with an advance copy of my first book, *My Badass Book of Saints*, and a religious visa to Cuba for the apostolic visit of Pope Francis. When I started writing that book in late 2014, I consecrated the project to Our Lady of Charity of El Cobre. Much of my personal story is told in that book, as well as a tribute to my devotion to the Blessed Virgin Mary under this title. As a Cuban-born daughter of Mary, it was a no-brainer I'd want to share her with my readers.

I never expected that within a year of making that consecration to Mary and renewing my commitment to Christ, I would be placing a copy of my book on the steps of the sanctuary in the Basilica Shrine of Our Lady of Charity of El Cobre—in Cuba!—moments after Pope Francis celebrated Mass there. I was moved to give her that gift in thanksgiving.

Mary's gift to me unfolded in the week that followed as I reconnected with family and my roots on a whirlwind trip west toward Havana. I visited places from my childhood and, more importantly, visited people with whom the bond of love was stronger than the chasm of distance and the passing of years.

I became acutely aware of Our Lady of Charity's presence throughout this adventure. She brought me there and then showered me with graces on the visit. I thought I had a strong devotion to Mary going into this trip. I returned not just confident and sure of her maternal care for me but closer than ever to her Son, our Lord Jesus Christ. More than anything, I felt love at every turn on this trip, as her name is Charity, or Love, and her Son is Love Incarnate.

Looking Back, Looking Forward

My initial devotion to Mary was largely an accident of birth. I was born in Cuba in the 1960s. My father was educated by the Marist Brothers. My mother was educated by the Teresian Sisters. I grew up in a home that was both devout and culturally sensitive to Marian devotion. Our Lady of Charity, the patroness of Cuba, was a natural influence in my life.

Whenever my mother referred to the Blessed Virgin Mary, she did so lovingly and with an affectionate diminutive, the *virgencita*. In this way, Mary was always present in our home, a part of the family.

I knew the Blessed Mother in the same intimate way I knew my grandparents, aunts, and uncles who lived far away and yet loved me dearly. I knew and loved my heavenly mother with a trust that was as innocent as my young years. But if you asked me why I felt so loved, or pressed me to explain who the virgencita is, I couldn't have done it. I would have delivered my response to why I felt so loved with conviction: "Because." I didn't have any other information to share.

Some fifty years later, I might give the same emphatic response: "Because!" Now, though, I can tell you why. Our Lady of Charity's story is filled with tradition, history, adventure, and, as her title suggests, love. I'd like to share it with you and invite you to get to know Mary under the title Our Lady of Charity.

This book is a labor of love that begins at a very personal level. As an immigrant to the United States, I've often lived in two worlds—my adopted country, to which I've sworn my allegiance as a naturalized citizen, and a nostalgic vision (and sometimes, specter) of the Cuba left behind by my parents and so many of their generation. I grew up embracing the opportunities available in our new home. We quickly adopted Uncle Sam as our *tío* and accepted everything he symbolized. At the same time, we retained a love of our *Cachita*, the virgencita so a part of our Cuban identity. My story as an immigrant and a pilgrim is a story of political freedom and religious freedom. It is a story about faith.

I'd like to share this story with my Cuban American brothers and sisters who love Our Lady of Charity but would like to know more about her beyond her appearance to the Three Juans.

I'd like to share her story with my children, nieces, and nephews and all the American-born second- and third-generation *cubanitos* who recognize Our Lady of Charity. She is so much more than a cultural icon: I want you to know who she is and how much she loves you.

I want to introduce Our Lady of Charity to her North American children. Devotion to Mary under this lovely title comes at a time when our society, and our world, should revisit her message of love. We can turn to the Blessed Virgin Mary as our model for living this call to love. She never fails to show us the true love of the Father, the Son, and the Holy Spirit.

1.

$\mathcal{M}$ARY RESCUES US FROM THE STORM

The Story of the Virgin of Charity

Oh sinner, be not discouraged but have recourse to Mary in all your necessities. Call her to your assistance, for such is the Divine Will that she should help in every kind of necessity.

—St. Basil the Great

A Stormy Flight

I returned to Cuba through the eastern province of Holguin. That is where Christopher Columbus made landfall and encountered this beautiful island known as the Pearl of the Antilles. It's where I sat, thousands of feet above the coastline, peering out of a tiny plane's window, hoping to catch a glimpse of the land below. Late afternoon had turned to evening, and the plane was bouncing about as we approached the airport in a storm. The turbulence outside causing the plane to jump was nothing compared to the atomic butterflies in my stomach. Nevertheless, the apprehension I felt about the unknown was soon replaced by excitement and then a calm acceptance of everything I was going to experience. The winds had abated by the time we landed, but a soft rain fell as we walked across the tarmac. I remember thinking it was as if stars were falling from the sky. The tarmac was poorly lit, but we could see the lights from the airport shine through the falling rain.

Our intrepid little group, my mother and her sisters and I, piled into a church van with my waiting uncles, and we were swept away into the Cuban night. Everyone was talking at once, but I was feeling a bit out of time—as if I was experiencing everything in slow motion. It's only in retrospect that I see the poetic connection: Mary returned me to Cuba, saving me from a storm and bringing me to the safety of loved ones I'd longed to see. It's what she does.

The Story of Our Lady of Charity

Some four hundred years earlier, along the same coast, heavy waves crashed against a little rowboat, terrifying the three men attempting to cross the Bay of Nipe, located in the eastern part of Cuba. The sudden storm caught them unprepared. Unable to get back to shore safely, and unlikely to ride out the storm without capsizing, they turned to the Blessed Virgin Mary in their anguish and fear, begging for her intercession.

The storm ceased, and the waters calmed. In those first few moments of relief as the men tried to compose themselves and steady their course, they saw something near the side of their boat. Thinking it was a piece of driftwood churned up in the storm, they looked closer. Their discovery would not only change their lives but be a witness and companion to a people and a nation in centuries to come.

The men pulled from the water a board with a small statue lashed to it. Along the board, they could see writing: *Yo soy la Virgen de la Caridad.* "I am the Virgin of Charity." The message confused them. They were not familiar with this title of Mary, but having just prayed for her intercession, they were certain this was a gift from heaven. Even more confusing, the board and the statue were not wet. The men were curious and perhaps a bit apprehensive. Convinced that the Blessed Mother had calmed the storm, they took the message of the statue as confirmation that Mary had in fact appeared to protect and care for her children.

Their safe return with the statue would launch decades of mystery, intrigue, and deep devotion. So powerful was the impact of this little statue's appearance that myths and legends quickly grew around its discovery and installation in Cuba. That little Lady of Charity tells a story about the indigenous people of Cuba, the African slaves working in the copper mines, and the Spanish settlers governing the island and its people.

But most of all, it tells a story about faith.

It was faith, after all, that saved the men.

A New Land and a New Evangelization

The story of faith and home that my family tells begins in the early years of the sixteenth century. The world was in turmoil. The world, it seems, is always in turmoil, ever since that fateful day in the Garden of Eden when Adam and Eve first sinned against God. Now Europe was facing a violent and deadly state of constant war with invading Saracen forces. Christianity was threatened, but the New World offered opportunities for evangelization. It was also a time of discovery and expansion into the Western Hemisphere, as Europeans explored the islands and continents they had not known existed.

The Spanish colonizers who settled in the Caribbean were often accompanied by Catholic missionaries. As a result, the newly established colonies tended to have vibrant religious structures in place, with churches and priests participating quite actively in the daily life of these settlements. The presence of the Church led to many conversions among the native peoples, as Dominican and Franciscan friars began the earliest education efforts through evangelization. When African slaves were brought to Cuba, evangelization efforts increased.

The Franciscans maintained a presence in Cuba for centuries. Two of my Spanish-Basque great-uncles served in Cuba as missionaries. One was a secular priest, and the other a Franciscan friar. The friar spent many years in Cuba, continuing the long tradition of his order. This tradition was part of a lovely family connection to Franciscans: I was born in the city of Santa Clara, named for St. Clare of Assisi, and I was baptized in a Franciscan parish that was, no doubt, the fruit of those early missionaries.

One of my favorite moments during my trip to Cuba was attending Mass in that church. Today, after years of atheism promoted by a Communist government, Franciscan friars have returned to resume the work of evangelization they began some four hundred years ago.

A Land in Need of Love

The intersection of Cuba's native people—the Arawak peoples (Taínos and Siboney)—the African slaves, and the Spaniards created a small melting pot in the settlement Santiago del Prado. The Spanish crown commissioned a royal mining entity to extract copper from this area rich in natural resources. To paint a picture of peaceful coexistence would be disingenuous. The native population was beset with disease and abuse through forced labor. The African slaves brought to supplement this workforce did not fare much better. Many attempted to escape to the mountains. Those who were not successful suffered under harsh conditions. Many perished. Thus, the labor force was in a constant state of replenishment from the slave trade.

Almost a century of this forced coexistence passed. By the early 1600s, Santiago del Prado was a bustling and productive center for copper mining. The royal mining company flourished under the management of Francisco Sanchez de Moya in the late 1500s and early 1600s. Sanchez de Moya believed in more benevolent care of the workers, and although they were still enslaved, they were given greater access to food and medical care. Some slaves were paid wages, and others were allowed the use of land to grow their own crops. Sanchez de Moya also made it possible for the friars to actively engage in evangelization, even designing a system for bringing these fledgling Christians to Mass. Meanwhile, devotion to the Blessed Mother was growing, too.

That Fateful Storm and the First Shrine

As a way to make the colony self-sustaining, the mining company expanded its reach to include farms and cattle. Many laborers worked in sugarcane fields, and others became cowhands. The business of slaughtering and preserving meat grew. Two Native American brothers, Rodrigo and Juan de Hoyos, were expert ranchers and adept at collecting the salt necessary for the preservation of the meat.

One day, Rodrigo and Juan went out to gather salt in the salt marshes of the Bay of Nipe. They took with them Juan Moreno, an African boy. That was the day they encountered the storm, invoked the protection of the Blessed Virgin Mary, and found the statue of Our Lady of Charity. The men returned by way of the town of Barajagua, where they took the small statue and built a shrine for veneration. They were moved by their experience and felt compelled to share their story.

The original statue was moved from Barajagua to a church in El Cobre as the devotion grew. A short time later, the statue disappeared from the church in El Cobre and reappeared—wet—at the shrine in Barajagua. This happened a number of times, and the locals believed that the Blessed Mother was indicating her desire to remain in the area where the statue was found. In a way, no matter where the statue was moved, she did remain there, as devotion to Our Lady of Charity continued to grow and spread in the area.

I visited Barajagua during my pilgrimage in 2015. The devotion to Our Lady of Charity that began there more than four hundred years ago still permeates the area today. I imagined myself traveling along the path the men took when they built that first shrine, a humble building made of palm fronds. Construction of a new shrine had just begun some months before I visited, but it was already a welcoming sanctuary from the dusty dirt highway and the business of life outside its walls. The new shrine was finished and dedicated in October of 2017, a fitting and beautiful moment in the history of the devotion as a replica of the original statue was enthroned above the altar. A life-sized replica of the statue also stood in front of the building, reminding all those traveling through town of Our Lady's presence—not just a historical reference but a reminder of the Blessed Virgin Mary's accompaniment of all of us as we journey through life.

Cachita, Our Mother

Eventually, the "disappearing" statue was placed in the small chapel of the hospital at the copper mines in Santiago del Prado. There, the veneration of Our Lady of Charity continued to grow. It was here that she would eventually be known by the title of Our Lady of Charity of El Cobre.

In 1687, Juan Moreno related the details of his adventure to an official court reporter for Church records. Marian devotion in the area had increased in the decades since that fateful day, and Moreno, now at an advanced age, recorded his whole experience for posterity. The statue was subsequently placed in numerous churches in the area until finally, in 1926, the beautiful National Shrine of Our Lady of Charity was built. It was elevated to a basilica on December 2, 1977.

Our Lady of Charity emerged from the depths of her children's need. Cubans saw in Mary, under this title, a mother to them all. It's important to note that in the hospital chapel, Our Lady of Charity was accessible to everyone working in the mines—no pilgrimage into the town to the cathedral was necessary. Mary was with her children. They needed her, and she was present. This reality, the presence of Mary through the ages, served as a consolation in those days and continues to comfort us today.

I've heard many nicknames for Our Lady of Charity, sweet diminutives full of affection, such as my mother's use of virgencita, "little virgin." Sometimes we use Cachita, derived from the Spanish Caridad, or "Charity." Frequently, she's called morenita, a description of her Creole complexion. The features on the statue are racially ambiguous, representative of the comingling of the various cultures in that area. Under this title of Our Lady of Charity, Mary drew the early Cubans to herself as her children and, thus, as brothers and sisters in Christ. Four centuries later, we still call her our mother.

My Virgencita

Perhaps the loveliest characteristic of Our Lady of Charity is that she teaches us about Jesus with her presence. Where Mary goes, there is Jesus, her Son. This is clear in the imagery we see in Our Lady of Charity. She holds her Son in one hand and the foreshadowing of his passion, a cross, in her other hand. Salvation history is held in her arms; we merely need to contemplate the image to see the Incarnation and the Passion.

Modern depictions of Our Lady of Charity show her rising above the turbulent seas, three men at her feet looking up to her. This image, engraved in the psyche of the Cuban people, has evolved over the centuries.

As word spread and locals came out to see this miraculous statue that survived a storm without getting wet, the story grew and the details were embellished.

While it's certain that a young African boy, Juan Moreno, was one of the occupants of the boat, the identities of the other two men evolved over the years, creating a subtly different narrative. Some artistic depictions show white Europeans or mixed-race men, in a desire to be inclusive of all of Mary's children. The men's identities morphed into the "Three Juans," although records indicate possibly only one or maybe two actually had that name. This subtle shift in the narrative coexists with the documented history contained in Church records. This new narrative reaffirms the Blessed Mother as a mother to all.

This is the image of the Blessed Mother that I know and the story I've heard, with variations here and there, throughout my life. When I pray for her intercession, I am on that boat with the Three Juans, looking up at her dazzling white robe and blue mantle the color of the sea. Her smile comforts and calms me.

My knowledge of faith and family, and even Cuban history, was taught and reinforced with extemporaneous oral histories inspired by whatever was happening in the moment. A familiar scent, a special meal, or a letter from Cuba became opportunities for joyful stories even as they were often tinged with melancholy. The story of Our Lady of Charity is intimately woven into my story alongside other family tales about shipbuilding and deep-sea fishing from my father, as well as my mother's descriptions of afternoons on the farm.

I relished my parents' recollections. Not only did they help me connect to relatives I knew only by name, but also they developed my identity with roots in Cuba, roots that were as much Catholic as familial and cultural. Those three aspects of my identity are one. To love my parents is to also love their Cuba, and to love Cuba is to love Our Lady of Charity. Or maybe it's the other way around. Love of family, love of our birthplace, and love of our faith are seen intimately in our devotion to Our Lady of Charity.

My earliest recollection of the virgencita, as we called the Virgin Mary when I was a child, was on holy cards with the image of a storm churning the waters and Mary above the waters, larger than life, bigger than the storm.

For a small child, that presence was greater than the detail of the men's facial features or whether they were in a rowboat or a canoe. What I learned at my mother's knee, as she told me about this beautiful woman and the child she held in her arms, was that there is a love greater than anything I understood. It was my earliest lesson about my Catholic faith. I understood my own mother's love, if not in words, then certainly in the feeling of safety and comfort in her arms. Perhaps the words my mother spoke were above my ability to comprehend at the time, but I understood that the men in the boat wanted that safety, too. They wanted to be with that baby, Jesus, safe in the arms of love.

I think most Cuban children who grew up seeing this image on holy cards or icons in churches and in the community received at some level this fundamental message of love. Mary's name is love, and she brings us Love Incarnate.

What I see when I gaze upon Our Lady of Charity is a refuge in the storm. My daily tasks don't take me out in unfriendly waters, but the challenge of

living in a world filled with physical and spiritual
dangers often sends me to my knees in prayer.

My Love of Mary Demands More from Me

My love of Our Lady of Charity opened my heart
and my eyes to Mary as intercessor. I learned to pray
the Rosary, and the more I prayed through the Joyful,
Luminous, Sorrowful, and Glorious Mysteries, the
deeper I was drawn into this devotion. I hungered
for more information about the graces obtained
through this centuries-old prayer.

Mary's constant presence in my life—whether as
Our Lady of Charity or under other titles—became
apparent to me as I got older. I can look back on my
life and make connections, see patterns, even see the
hand of God leading and opening the way for me.
I'm especially delighted when I find Mary's influence during a time I wasn't aware of it.

Apparently, the Blessed Mother was sowing
the seeds of my love of the Rosary in the unlikeliest
of places: the basketball court! I played basketball
throughout elementary and high school. As Catholic
students, we started each game with a prayer. The
prayer varied from year to year and coach to coach,
but we ended it the same way: *Our Lady of Victory,
pray for us!* I prayed that dozens and dozens of times
but never knew the story of Our Lady of Victory.
Imagine my surprise to discover I knew her as Our
Lady of the Rosary!

Our Lady of Victory reminds me of the powerful
graces and the protection of the Rosary. In 1571, Pope
Pius V exhorted all of Rome to take to the churches,

day and night, and pray the Rosary for the protection of the European coastal cities from the invading forces of the Ottoman Empire. A great sea battle in the Mediterranean, known as the Battle of Lepanto, ensued. The Ottoman navy was defeated, and in thanksgiving, Pius V commemorated the date, October 7, as the feast day of Our Lady of Victory. In this instance of turmoil and danger, the faithful found succor in the calming familiarity of the Rosary, especially when recited in a group.

Today we have recourse to the Blessed Mother through the very same Rosary—a prayer that both comforts and instructs. Many saints have lauded the benefits of the Holy Rosary. St. Padre Pio said of this devotion, "Some people are so foolish that they think they can go through life without the help of the Blessed Mother. Love the Madonna and pray the Rosary, for her Rosary is the weapon against the evils of the world today. All graces given by God pass through the Blessed Mother."[1]

The rosary is a sacramental, an object that helps us express our piety—it is not a lucky charm that we use to invoke magic. The prayers, when recited with reverence, draw us close to Christ through meditation. It is powerful precisely because the Rosary draws us into holiness. We join ourselves to Mary, who is our mediator and intercessor.

St. John Paul II had a deep devotion to the Blessed Virgin Mary, and thus a deep devotion to the prayers of the Rosary. In the introduction to his apostolic letter *Rosarium Virginis Mariae* (*On the Most Holy Rosary*), he instructs us:

The Rosary of the Virgin Mary, which gradu-
ally took form in the second millennium under
the guidance of the Spirit of God, is a prayer
loved by countless saints and encouraged by
the Magisterium. Simple yet profound, it still
remains, at the dawn of this third millennium,
a prayer of great significance, destined to bring
forth a harvest of holiness. It blends easily into
the spiritual journey of the Christian life, which,
after two thousand years, has lost none of the
freshness of its beginnings and feels drawn by
the Spirit of God to "set out into the deep" (*duc
in altum!*) in order once more to proclaim, and
even cry out, before the world that Jesus Christ
is Lord and Savior, "the way, and the truth and
the life" (Jn 14:6), "the goal of human history
and the point on which the desires of history
and civilization turn."[2]

To know that a beloved saint such as John Paul
II exhorts me to embrace this prayer encourages me
not only to learn more about the Rosary and to make
every effort to recite it with piety and reverence but
also to open myself to other devotions. Our faith
is rich with sacramentals, expressions of faith that
bring us closer to holiness. I don't think I would
have picked up that rosary in my thirties if I hadn't,
in some way, been fostering a relationship with the
Blessed Mother through my devotion to Our Lady
of Charity of El Cobre. She, in turn, gently but insis-
tently fostered in me a relationship with her Son,
Jesus Christ, through the beauty of the Holy Rosary.
As St. John Paul II reminds us, "To pray the Rosary

is to hand over our burdens to the merciful hearts of Christ and his Mother."[3]

Praying the Rosary reinforces for me how desperately we need grace—not just the kind of grace that saves us from physical harm, as the Three Juans prayed for deliverance in the storm, but also the grace that protects us from serious spiritual dangers to our souls.

Prayer

Our Lady of Charity, I turn to you in the storm of anxiety and chaos swirling around me, confident you will calm the waters of confusion and unrest.

Like the Three Juans who implored your intercession, I place myself under your protection.

Show me your radiant smile filled with love. Comfort me, as I gaze upon the cross in your right hand and the infant Jesus under your heart, a reminder that Innocence assumed our sins on the Cross and, in one more act of love, gave you to us, our mother.

Thank you, Lord, for this beautiful gift of your mother. An intercessor, a model, a beacon in the storm that guides us to a safe harbor in you. Amen.

2.

MARY EMBRACES THE DIGNITY OF HER CHILDREN

The Colonial Period

The Blessed Virgin is like a good mother who, not content with looking after all her children in general, watches over each one separately.

—St. John Vianney

Mary Seeks Us

When I think of Mary and the Visitation, I can't help but smile. So much is happening in that encounter. On the surface, Mary is visiting her cousin in what would surely be a lovely stay filled with joy and laughter, support and comfort, and very likely work and sacrifice to help Elizabeth get ready for the birth of her long-awaited child.

But that view barely scratches the surface. Mary is, in this moment, the first evangelist, someone who brings the message and love of Christ to others, as she brings Jesus to her cousin's household. This intimate scene, small as it seems, is actually explosive in its scope. Elizabeth's baby leaps in her womb! Elizabeth declares her wonder and joy as she and her child are touched by the Holy Spirit! "When Elizabeth heard Mary's greeting, the infant leaped in her womb, and Elizabeth, filled with the holy Spirit, cried out in a loud voice and said, 'Most blessed are you among women, and blessed is the fruit of your womb. And how does this happen to me, that the mother of my Lord should come to me? For at the moment the sound of your greeting reached my ears, the infant in my womb leaped for joy'" (Lk 1:41–44).

I didn't always have an appreciation for the magnitude of this encounter, but ever since I truly understood Mary as the first to know and love Jesus and bring him into the world, my response to her has become more and more like Elizabeth's, full of wonder and joy. To encounter the Blessed Virgin Mary is to encounter Christ, after all.

This is beautifully captured in Mary's presence to the Three Juans under the title of Our Lady of Charity. She came to their aid when they were caught in the storm, surprised them with a tangible sign of her presence, and then remained with them, not just through the storm but afterward in their lives. Mary moved them so much that they set out to build a shrine and share the wonder of their encounter. That's the part of the story we need to understand fully. Mary is present to us, always. When the men prayed for her assistance, she calmed the sea, but she also made her presence known to them in a way they would understand and remember.

This statue that appeared miraculously in the water, dry in spite of the stormy waves, tells a powerful story of salvation. Our Lady of Charity, as the statue proclaims, carries Christ in one arm and the symbol of his passion and death in the other. Mary's presence to the men not only saves them in their moment of peril at sea but also evangelizes them.

The tangible presence of the statue gave the men a sign for their own conviction and proof to bring back to their village and share with the people. The African slaves as well as the native peoples of Cuba had been receiving instruction in the faith for decades, but the task of genuine conversion posed a challenge as the Christian faith competed with indigenous animistic worship and deities brought from Africa. The statue of the Blessed Mother could have been confused with these goddesses, except that she clearly represented the Mother of God in this most amazing presence of the infant Jesus and the Cross.

Veneration of the Blessed Mother in the little shrine for Our Lady of Charity was a subtle but effective evangelization: to look upon her is to be reminded of our salvation.

Thus began a relationship with the Cuban people that spans centuries. Our Lady of Charity's presence is felt today anywhere her children are isolated, in exile, or find themselves in a stormy world filled with unknown physical and spiritual dangers.

The Gift of Presence

When Christ spoke from the Cross to the beloved disciple, John, commending Mary to his care, he gave to us the gift of his own mother: "When Jesus saw his mother and the disciple there whom he loved, he said to his mother, 'Woman, behold, your son.' Then he said to the disciple, 'Behold, your mother.' And from that hour the disciple took her into his home" (Jn 19:26–27).

This powerful scene shows more than a good son providing for the care of his mother. The Church sees this as the moment when Jesus Christ gave us his own mother as ours. Mary has not only been a loving mother to her Son; she has also been Christ's first and preeminent disciple. Mary as our heavenly mother is more than an advocate, a source of consolation or hope. In the Blessed Mother we have the consummate teacher. When we call upon her to come to our aid, she comes, as good mothers do. And Mary leads us through her example to the source of all love, her Son, Jesus Christ.

This gift of both presence and direction envelops the devotees of Our Lady of Charity of El Cobre. The Blessed Mother's patronage of the Cuban people under this title beautifully addresses the imminent need of her three children in the boat, but the miracle of her loving presence and intercession is also seen in the devotion to her that developed during the formation of a fledgling nation. How fitting that she be present at this crossroads in the New World and, greater still, that the image venerated include her Son, Jesus Christ!

The Three Juans took their story of miraculous intervention and the subsequent finding of this virgencita to the people in their community. As word of these wonders spread, so too did the work of evangelization. Everyone who turned to Our Lady of Charity for aid or for prayers encountered her Son.

The Blessed Mother's Presence during the Colonial Period

Spain's occupation of Cuba began in 1492 when Christopher Columbus landed on the northeastern coast in what is today known as the province of Holguin. By 1511, Diego Velázquez de Cuéllar formed the first Spanish settlement in Baracoa. The Spanish colonization of Cuba in the 1500s followed a pattern of violence and oppression of the indigenous peoples sadly common in the settling of the Americas. The island's inhabitants were ill equipped to defend themselves from disease and armed colonists, and they retreated into the mountains or were captured and indentured for the work of the settlements. These small coastal settlements were often attacked from the sea by buccaneers and pirates from other European nations, especially the French and English.

By the 1600s, Cuba was a conquered land. The indigenous population was decimated. African slaves had been introduced. An uneasy coexistence was developing at the intersection of three lands—Europe, Africa, and the Caribbean. In short, it was a land roiling with undercurrents of turmoil and, despite missionaries working to evangelize in Cuba, desperately in need of God's saving grace.

It was into this storm that Mary entered in 1612, carrying with her the Good News of salvation.

The late 1600s would see a dramatic increase in both faith and devotion. News of Our Lady of Charity traveled quickly from Barajagua to Santiago, and devotion to Mary under this title grew throughout the eastern part of Cuba. In many cases, Our Lady of Charity became an introduction to the Catholic faith for the Africans and Native Americans living in Cuba. The Blessed Mother, ever the evangelist, introduced her Cuban children to her Son. Although the Catholic missionaries moved among the settlements and did important work, it was the Three Juans, in their zeal and great devotion, who built the very first little shrine in the heart of their community for their people. For some in this community, learning about the Mother of God came first and was an introduction to her Son, our Lord Jesus Christ.

This first shrine was deeply meaningful to the indigenous people, as they felt the Blessed Mother had come to them, specifically. The statue was kept in Barajagua for a time, but as word of this devotion spread to Santiago, the statue was moved, by church officials, to the parish church in El Cobre. The statue would stay in El Cobre for a time, and then disappear and reappear at the shrine in Barajagua. Legends say the statue would appear on the altar, wet, as if it had traveled through water. Some say the disappearances and reappearances were miraculous.[1]

Finally, the statue found a permanent home in El Cobre. More conversions and baptisms followed. Soon, miracles were attributed to Our Lady of

Charity. The first miraculous intervention happened shortly after the statue was moved to El Cobre. Matthias de Olivera, a hermit who dedicated himself to the care of the shrine of Our Lady of Charity in Santiago del Prado, often led the laborers from the mines in prayer. One day, he fell down a mine shaft. He would have fallen to his death but was miraculously caught on a vine and managed to hold on until he was rescued by the workers. Olivera attributed his survival to the intercession of Our Lady of Charity.

The mid-1600s were fraught with changes that challenged the success of the mining company as well as the agricultural and ranching endeavors that provided for the growing community of laborers. Sanchez de Moya's legacy of respect for the laborers, his approach for a self-sustaining community, and support of church evangelization—all of which led to a thriving community—were rejected by new leadership in the mines. Production was significantly reduced due in large part to mismanagement. The growing city of Havana on the west side of the island also turned to closer sources of metals and other resources, reducing the need for output in El Cobre. The community suffered for it.

Havana was becoming more influential and was a strategic location for launching expeditions as well as trade into the Gulf of Mexico. As Cuba's capital, Havana quickly became the center of influence. It naturally followed that the Church would transfer the bishop, and the see, to Havana.

To the inhabitants of El Cobre, it looked like the Spanish had abandoned them, but the Blessed

Mother, Our Lady of Charity, remained present to her children. When a hurricane destroyed the parish church and little shrine, a new shrine was erected in 1655, this one explicitly for Our Lady of Charity. Her children knew their mother and wanted her close. For those who lived and worked in El Cobre, the connection to this little *morenita*, dark-skinned virgin, grew stronger.

The late 1600s experienced a revival of the mining industry, but the port city of Santiago suffered attacks from English and French pirates and privateers. The invasion of Jamaica, a Spanish colony, by the English and the subsequent migration of Spanish Jamaicans to Santiago created a new dynamic, and a power struggle ensued. No longer merely a colony, the island started to experience migration from other places. Each wave of migration brought with it new populations and new hearts and souls to be converted.

The 1700s saw more skirmishes and armed aggression in Santiago and Havana, particularly from the British. In fact, periodic invasions by the British took Santiago de Cuba and Guantanamo Bay in the middle part of the century; even Havana was invaded, with British forces occupying the city for a year before agreeing to withdraw in 1763.

The peace treaty between the Spanish and British gave up Florida to the British, but the changes that were introduced in Cuba during the British occupation had a lasting effect on the direction of Cuba's development. Trade expanded during that time into North America, and the economy took an upswing that resulted in rapid growth. Sadly, thousands more African slaves were introduced into Cuba, too. African slaves had been an early part of the Spanish settlements, but Spanish trade restrictions severely curtailed the importing of slaves. After the English rescinded these restrictions, the slave trade opened aggressively and continued for decades.

Despite these growths and setbacks, by the 1800s, Our Lady of Charity was deeply rooted in the spiritual and cultural lives of the Cuban people, and the devotion continued to spread. Cuba had developed its national identity. The Spanish and African influences, combined with that of the native peoples, produced a vibrant new culture. This new nation produced artists, architects, philosophers, writers, businessmen, and of course, politicians. The Catholic Church in Cuba officially recognized devotion to Mary under the title Our Lady of Charity. Cachita, as she was lovingly called, or *morenita*, a reference to her Creole complexion, spoke to all Cubans, whether Spanish, African, or Creole. The rest, as they say, is history.

My Encounter with Cachita in Barajagua

Today, the road from Holguin to Santiago is as busy a thoroughfare as it was in Cuba's early days. In 2015, I visited the town where the first little shrine to Our Lady of Charity stood, originally a chapel made of palm fronds in the style of the indigenous people of the area. I met the team of three laborers who worked in the September heat, laying tile inside a new shrine under construction. The building is a good-sized chapel, at once spacious and intimate. Anyone who passes by knows it is a shrine to Our Lady of Charity as a life-sized statue of her stands outside the building, smiling at travelers as she shows them her Son, Jesus, in her arms.

As a Cuban-born American, I was moved to pilgrimage here and stand in wonder as this little church took shape. A lot has transpired in this area, and throughout Cuba, since Our Lady of Charity was first venerated here. On this day, I was just another traveler on this journey.

My family and I were following the route Juan Moreno and his companions took after retrieving the miraculous little statue from the waters of the bay. The Bay of Nipe is in the province of Holguin, where we started our pilgrimage. Our stop in Barajagua was brief but personally and spiritually moving nonetheless. Modern cars zoomed past, but out here in the countryside, I also saw horse-drawn wagons and donkeys being led along the road. People walked with a purpose, and some neighbors from nearby homes came out to their stoops, maybe to watch our little pilgrim group exit the cramped church van, maybe to just watch the bustling movement along the road. There was nothing else to see there, but I wanted to see it all.

I felt both a stranger in a strange land and oddly at home. My sneakers and jeans probably gave me away as an American. But my accent and fluency in colloquial Spanish surprised and disarmed those I met.

Inside of the shrine it's cool, and the men expertly laid tile in what would be the sacristy. There was a makeshift altar made of wooden boards, but I saw signs that Mass had been celebrated there; a crucifix lay flat on the tabletop. A small replica of Our Lady of Charity sat on a shelf behind the altar. Everywhere I went in Cuba, I spied Cachita—on a shelf, in a painting, or sometimes on a poster. Seeing this statue in the shrine reminded me that the devotion to the Blessed Virgin Mary began here. Here! The realization moved me. The men were building a new spiritual home in the community where it all began, and the sense of history was palpable.

As I looked out toward the front door, I noticed three pallets made up as beds. The men lived there while they worked. I was humbled by their dedication and need. There are no hotels on that stretch of highway. They worked and lived in the church as they built it. Just as Juan Moreno and the Hoyos brothers must have done four hundred years ago, these men lovingly prepared a place for the Lord and his mother.

I spoke with them a little, not wanting to interrupt their work for too long, but they joyfully gave me a brief tour. I could see their pride in their workmanship—not a boastful pride in their skill but rather a sweet humility in giving 100 percent of their craft to Cachita. What a gift to work with such joy!

This beautiful church, now finished, was dedicated on October 14, 2017. The sanctuary is ready to receive pilgrims on their way to El Cobre. The statue of Our Lady of Charity beckons travelers to come in and rest from their journey, but it is our Lord residing in the tabernacle that welcomes them inside.

Several years have passed since I was first in that church, side by side with the men building it. I've pondered that scene often, blessed by the opportunity to experience vicariously these sons' love and service to their heavenly mother and the grace manifest in their joy to be working, to be serving a purpose greater than themselves.

We might say history repeats itself in this scene, but I think the truth is something greater. God's love, and Mary's, is not just eternal; it is also timeless. Our Lady of Charity loved her sons four hundred years ago, and today, and always. It's a love for me, too. And you.

Small Steps

Growing up in a part of the United States that had few Catholics made me a little defensive when it came to talking about the Blessed Virgin Mary and the saints. Inevitably, I'd find myself in a situation where I'd have to defend myself and the faith. "No," I'd say, "we don't worship Mary. No. We don't worship saints." My soul sighed every time.

I felt ill equipped for apologetics. I wasn't confident about my ability to refer to scripture, so I didn't really want to engage in a deep conversation. Nevertheless, I did try to explain why praying to Mary and the saints, in addition to praying to God the Father, Son, and Holy Spirit, enriches our prayer life and gives us hope and consolation, among other graces.

I'd go on to explain my relationship with the saints in the way many of us have done—by describing them as friends in heaven or on earth whom we entreat for prayers. I don't know that I even convinced anyone—that's a job for the Holy Spirit—but I'm sure I made them pause and think.

I have venerated many saints in my life. I've been blessed by opportunities to travel abroad and in the United States, and during my travels I've visited churches, shrines, and other holy places. I've prayed before altars, relics, and icons in an effort to bring my heart and mind closer to the models of holiness before me. Some saints have attracted me in much the same way friends have, and I have become devoted to them in the way I became devoted to my acquaintances. As the *Catechism of the Catholic Church* expresses, devotions like these enhance our spiritual life: "The religious sense of the Christian people has always found expression in various forms of piety surrounding the Church's sacramental life, such as the veneration of relics, visits to sanctuaries, pilgrimages, processions, the stations of the cross, religious dances, the rosary, medals, etc." (*CCC*, 1674).

My visit to Barajagua and El Cobre affected me profoundly. I have venerated the Blessed Mother under many titles, especially Our Lady of Charity. I've often said I have a special devotion to this *virgencita*. However, my pilgrimage to Barajagua and the Basilica Shrine in El Cobre ignited my heart not just with a deeper love for the Blessed Mother but with a burning desire to share this devotion because of how beautifully she shares Jesus with us. In her arms we see our Savior, Jesus Christ.

Prayer

Our Lady of Charity, be present to me throughout my day. Be a companion, a helpmate, a guardian, but most of all, be my sweet mother.

I share with you my accomplishments, my joys, my fears, even my failures. I place myself at your mercy and care.

Teach me to love.

Shower me with the grace to offer my whole being to your Son, our Lord Jesus Christ. Amen.

3.

PATRONESS OF CUBA

The Virgen Mambisa

The greatest Saints, those richest in grace
and virtue will be the most assiduous in
praying to the Most Blessed Virgin, looking
up to her as the perfect model to imitate and
as a powerful helper to assist them.

—St. Louis Marie de Montfort

Models of Love for the Blessed Virgin Mary

Although I was born in Cuba, I came to the United
States at such a young age that I have few actual
memories of my birthplace. My childhood, however,
was filled with rich and beautiful stories told by my
parents, grandparents, aunts, and uncles. I know
this means that, oftentimes, those memories were
embellished or sweetened by nostalgia.

I may have rolled my eyes a time or two (let's
be honest, many times) when hearing those stories,
but I believe the greater truth of them—that their

beloved Cuba was a beautiful place, a wonderful home—even if some of the details were inconsistent or gilded. The truth is, I loved to hear these stories. They gave me a sense of family history, a connection to my identity as a daughter of Cuba, and a look into my family's faith.

My grandfather Alejandro was a man of few words, but his love of the ocean would animate him. When describing the ocean, he used the romantic feminine construction of the word, *la mar*, rather than the common *el mar*, which always sounded wrong to my ears because of his preference. As I grew older, I recognized that using *la mar* was his poetic way of expressing his deep love for the sea. The son of a ship's carpenter, he grew up surrounded by ship-builders. Saltwater coursed through his veins as surely as blood. While he had lived around the sea his entire life, he hadn't had the same influence in the practical matters of the faith. My grandfather's greatest gift to my grandmother was joining RCIA to complete his sacraments. He was baptized as an infant but was never confirmed. He was able to receive the sacraments before the renewal of their vows on their fiftieth wedding anniversary, when they also had their marriage convalidated in the Church.

His wife, my grandmother Amparo, attributed this blessing to the Blessed Mother's intercession. Her devotions and faith were part of her person. I remember that she never made plans, whether to go to a party or to the corner market for milk, without first saying, *Si Dios quiere*, "If God wills it." In this way, I grew up understanding that God had a plan for me, no matter how insignificant the details might appear.

My father had an understated faith, but it ran deep. He prayed the Rosary every day, and in his later years, he also developed a devotion to the Divine Mercy. When I discovered his full name, Vicente Alejandro de la Caridad, I teased him about it because Caridad—"Charity"—I thought, was a girl's name. I realized later that he had been consecrated to Our Lady of Charity. I wish I had understood this sooner; the idea of consecrating a child to the Blessed Mother never occurred to me until much later in my life. Most of the stories he told about Cuba featured his adventures in the schoolyard, playing baseball, or swimming in the harbor in Cienfuegos. Of course, he had tales, and tall tales, about swimming among the ships his grandfather had helped build. These stories gave us a taste of his carefree childhood. When we were older, some of the stories were more serious, but he spoke little of political upheaval. He had lived it and chose not to pass along the trauma.

My mother's stories were very different from my father's, but they were just as engaging. Her parents, my grandparents Daniel and Emilia, were Spanish Basques who fled Spain during the Spanish Civil War and settled in Cuba. My mother became a first-generation Cuban! As children of immigrants, she and I share many of the same experiences, although varied by different cultures. A natural storyteller, she taught me most of what I know about Cuban culture and history. My Basque grandparents were very devout;

their faith was implicitly experienced in their family life. As a result, my mother's stories tended to have a lesson woven in them. There's no better way to cultivate a moral character.

For us Cuban Americans, stories from our parents and grandparents were often the best connection we had to our Cuban heritage. My dearest friend from high school developed a trivia board game with her siblings called Ay Mi Cuba, "Oh My Cuba." They named the game after an expression their grandmother used: part lament, part sigh, part longing for the old days. It was a multigenerational game that covered Cuban history, language, popular culture, and idioms; it even included the Cuban American experience in Miami. The game was fun but impossible to win alone. Mostly, it opened up the gaming party to an evening of reminiscing and storytelling.

My friend perfectly captured how so much of the Cuban part of our identity comes from the stories our elders told. We learned the language, the music, and the customs from them. They instilled in us both an appreciation for our past in Cuba and a love of our country, the United States. It wasn't easy for them to see us slipping away—first the language, then the traditions. I'm sure that what I'm describing is a common experience for first-generation Americans, regardless of their origins. In the United States, I sometimes felt like a fish out of water, too Cuban in my customs to fit in comfortably. I mean, I dated with a chaperone. Yes. My mother once squeezed into the back seat of a 1977 Trans Am so I could go

to the movies with a nice Cuban American boy. It's
not that I didn't want to date American boys; I just
didn't want to explain my mother in the back seat. I
understand now that our parents and grandparents
wanted us to know where we came from, our history,
our identity as Cubans, but most importantly, how
our faith defined us. Our Lady of Charity became a
symbol of all those things.

Family was the source of everything, providing
for our basic needs, our education, and our faith.
Of all the crimes perpetrated by the Castro regime,
the most damaging was how the regime broke apart
families. This fracture in the family dynamic was
often the result not of animosity but rather of the
chasm of distance and blocked communication. How
I would have loved a relationship with my grandparents Daniel and Emilia! Nevertheless, I was blessed
to know them through my mother's stories and a
brief vacation with them in Miami. They knew what
it meant to be in exile, having experienced their own
escape from Spain. In my family, we have two generations that have fled their homeland. It's a deep
wound.

It's true that Cuban Americans feel the sting of
exile, passed on to us by our parents, but at the same
time we recognize this as part of the human condi-
tion. As Cuban Americans, we probably don't know
Cuban history as well as American history. But what
we do know is that Our Lady of Charity of El Cobre,
our heavenly mother, has always been with us and
always will be. Our parents and grandparents left

everything behind in Cuba, but they didn't leave behind the Blessed Mother.

We may know our personal family histories, some of us may have been drilled on the history of Cuba, but our relationship with Our Lady of Charity has been such a part of our cultural landscape that sometimes we forget who she is.

We would do well to see her in her heavenly glory, the Mother of God. The spouse of the Holy Spirit. The Mother of Mercy. The Cause of Our Joy. Co-Redemptorist. Mary has many titles. Relating her story as Our Lady of Charity naturally follows my desire to know about my family and my birthplace.

Patroness of a New Nation

Those first hundred or so years of colonization and development of Cuba were accompanied by this presence of Our Lady of Charity to the faithful. Marian devotion grew alongside the growth of the country.

Devotion to the Blessed Mother under this title began in a setting of profound depression and poverty. Mary's presence through the devotion of the Cuban Creoles, the descendants of the Arawak people, African slaves, and Spanish colonists became a source of consolation and catechesis, but on a wider scope, her presence serves a constant reminder that Mary remains by our side, accompanying us as we carry our crosses just as she accompanied Christ during his passion. Mary never left her Son's side, and in this life, Mary never leaves our side. We have an advocate in the Blessed Mother. Our struggles at work, within our families, and in our communities can be shared with the Blessed Virgin Mary. No trial is too small or too large for our mother.

Whatever we might say about the depth or breadth of evangelization and catechesis at that time, there is no doubt this devotion and love of the Mother of God grew from the seeds of faith present in those early Cuban Creoles in Barajagua and El Cobre. For the Cuban people entering a new era in the 1700s, Our Lady of Charity's unofficial but ever-present patronage would be called upon in a time ripe with hostilities, from pirates, buccaneers, and invading forces from Spain's enemies in Europe.

The turn of the nineteenth century saw increasing hostilities, especially from the French and English. Trade in sugarcane, tobacco, and, tragically, slaves continued to flourish. Cuba in the nineteenth century was looking a lot like the rest of the New World: settlement had given way to colonization and finally to development of a national identity.

My parents and grandparents often said that pre-Castro Cuba was similar to the United States. Cuba's history—both the negative aspects, such as slavery continuing into the late 1800s, and the positive, such as the country becoming a leading force in trade with North America and the rest of the Caribbean—was not unlike the European colonization happening to the north. However, unlike the North American colonies, often steeped in Protestant ideology, the Spanish colonies had no separation of church and state. The development of a national Cuban identity was affected as much by the Catholic

faith as it was by social, cultural, and political influences. At the heart of it, literally and figuratively,
was Our Lady of Charity of El Cobre, carrying her
message of love.

La Virgen Mambisa—A Patroness for Independence

The Virgin of Charity, a religious phenomenon, also
developed as a national and cultural phenomenon
as this devotion spread and grew among the Cuban
people. An emerging sense of Cuban nationalism in
the 1800s led to a widespread desire for independence from Spain. In 1868, with a cry for independence called the Grito de Yara, a Cuban landowner
named Carlos Manuel de Céspedes, frustrated by
planning and waiting for the right moment, freed
all his slaves and, in a bold move, started the war
for independence from Spain. This effort, known as
the Ten Years' War, failed. The Cubans tried again in
1880 and were squelched within months. However,
the desire remained, and the cause was picked up
again in the 1890s by José Martí, a man revered today
as a patriot and a renaissance man. By 1895, Cuba
was at war with Spain again. The United States had
economic and political interests in the outcome and
entered the war in 1898.

As an American student, I learned about this
as the Spanish-American War and recognized
two iconic incidents, the sinking of the USS *Maine*
in Havana's harbor and Teddy Roosevelt and his
Rough Riders charging San Juan Hill and defeat-
ing the Spanish. However, my Cuban background

taught me that this was first a war of Cuban independence from Spain before it was a war between
Spain and America. Before the Rough Riders there
were the Mambises—companies of Cuban freedom
fighters that had fought in the earliest attempts at
independence and gained strength in this war. They
were courageous men (and women!) who fought
with heart and little else, as they had no weapons
but the machetes that were their agricultural tools.
There were no supplies or food available beyond
what they could muster. But they were Cuban. And
they had their Cachita, who had been caring for her
Cuban children since the earliest days of this nation.

The Mambises, the freedom fighters, turned to
Our Lady of Charity and petitioned their mother
for help in their cause. She became an inspiration,
their own Virgen Mambisa. The first battle flag was
a banner Carlos Manuel de Céspedes had for a statue
of the Virgin. The Mambises consecrated themselves
and their cause to Our Lady of Charity and carried
medals and other tokens of their devotion to her.
Confident that Mary's intervention was responsible
for freeing the slaves in El Cobre in 1831, the Mambises turned to her to help free a nation.

Although the Americans helped defeat Spain,
thus ending the war, Cuban freedom wasn't exactly
achieved, even though there was a Cuban government established that was ready to rule. The United
States occupied Cuba, and it was the American flag
that flew victorious in Havana. It would take some
time before the government was turned over to the
new Republic of Cuba. In 1915, veterans of Cuba's

War of Independence—many of them Mambises, and all of them patriots—who still held a vision of a united nation wanted the new republic to officially recognize the Virgin of Charity as a symbol of unity because of her intercession and presence in the hearts and minds of the Cuban people. From the earliest days of devotion to Our Lady of Charity, the Cuban people felt they had an advocate, a mother, in her. Now, at the cusp of a new era for Cuba, the veterans believed she would be a source of reconciliation between Cubans who had fought for freedom and those who were loyal to Spain in these postwar years.

The veterans of the War of Independence appealed to the pope to make Our Lady of Charity the official patroness of Cuba. On May 10, 1916, Pope Benedict XV, by decree of the Sacred Congregation of Rites, proclaimed the Virgin of Charity of El Cobre as the patron saint of Cuba. Some decades later, the archbishop of Santiago de Cuba, the archdiocese where the National Basilica Shrine of Our Lady of Charity is located, requested a canonical coronation of the Virgin of Charity. This was granted December 20, 1936, by Pope Pius XI, and the archbishop held the coronation in Santiago in 1937.

Pope John Paul II formally carried out the papal coronation in Santiago de Cuba on January 24, 1998, during his apostolic visit. In his homily, he made reference not only to the great sacrifices made toward Cuba's independence from Spain but also to the spirit of the Cuban people:

From her shrine, not far from here, the Queen and Mother of all Cubans—regardless of race, political allegiance, or ideology—guides and sustains, as in times past, the steps of her sons and daughters towards our heavenly homeland, and she encourages them to live in such a way that *in society those authentic moral values may reign* which constitute the rich spiritual heritage received from your forebears. With gratitude, we turn to her, as did her cousin Elizabeth, and say: *"Blessed is she who believed that there would be a fulfilment of what was spoken to her by the Lord"* (Lk 1:45). In these words lies the secret of the true happiness of individuals and peoples: to believe and proclaim that the Lord has done marvelous things for us and that his mercy is from generation to generation on those who are faithful to him. This conviction is the force which inspires men and women to commit themselves selflessly, even at the cost of sacrifice, to the service of others.[1]

Three Popes: Models of Devotion to the Blessed Mother

Pope John Paul II's love of the Blessed Virgin Mary is well known. He dedicated his pontificate to Mary, and his apostolic motto, *Totus Tuus* ("Totally Yours"), speaks to his personal consecration to Mary. Here is a man, a saint, who understood reverence for Mary and the deep devotion Cubans have to Our Lady of Charity. John Paul II did more than recognize the importance of Our Lady of Charity to Cubans; during a general audience following his visit to Cuba, he spoke about the fracture that exists between Cubans who fled Communism and those who remained:

> In Santiago de Cuba, the primatial see, my visit became a real pilgrimage: there I knelt before the patroness of the Cuban people, Our Lady of Charity of El Cobre. I noticed with deep joy and emotion how much Cubans love the Mother of God, and how Our Lady of Charity is truly, over and above every difference, the principal symbol and support of the Cuban people's faith and their struggle for freedom. In this setting of popular piety, I urged them to incarnate the Gospel, the message of authentic liberation, in their daily lives by living as Christians fully involved in society. A hundred years ago, the country's independence was declared at the feet of Our Lady of Charity. With this pilgrimage I have entrusted to her care all Cubans, in their homeland and abroad, so that they may form a truly prosperous and fraternal community more and more enlivened by authentic freedom.[2]

The coronation, of course, was a significant symbol of how important this devotion is to the Cuban people. John Paul II's words and the fulfillment of the coronation remain powerful statements about the presence of the Blessed Mother in the Cuban heart. John Paul II adorned Our Lady of Charity with a beautiful gold crown and placed a gold rosary in the infant Jesus' hands.

This first apostolic visit to Cuba meant a great deal to the Cuban people and the Church, too. There were hopes for significant change within the country—policy changes that would improve human rights, economic possibilities, and, of course, promote religious freedom. Twenty years have passed since Pope John Paul II said, during his welcome in Cuba, "May Cuba, with all its magnificent possibilities, open itself to the world, and may the world open itself to Cuba."[3] A lot has happened since that first visit when John Paul II called himself a "messenger of truth and hope." Since then, two more popes have visited this island nation. As a Cuban American, I think that's pretty cool.

As a "pilgrim of charity," Pope Benedict XVI visited Cuba March 26–29, 2012. The three-day trip included the celebration of a papal Mass in Santiago to mark the four hundredth anniversary of the finding of the statue of the Virgin of Charity. Fourteen years after Pope John Paul II's historic visit, Pope Benedict's visit marked yet another milestone. He arrived in the midst of the jubilee year celebrating Our Lady of Charity after almost two years of public processions throughout Cuba with the statue of the Virgin of Charity. I imagine the papal Mass was a highlight in the year-long celebration of Cuba's devotion to the Blessed Mother.

The pope's presence was certainly a gift for the Cuban people, but he brought with him a gift for Our Lady of Charity: the Golden Rose of Christianity. The Golden Rose is a beautiful symbol that expresses both love and gratitude. The tradition of the rose dates back to the Middle Ages. Pope Benedict has given this gift to honor persons and to honor

the Blessed Virgin Mary at various shrines throughout the world. The rose, it is said, symbolizes Christ's
passion, both the beauty and the pain of the sacrifice.
What a poignant acknowledgment for Cachita and
the Cuban people, as Our Lady of Charity already
holds both in her arms!

When Pope Francis visited Cuba as a "missionary of mercy" in 2015, the theme of his apostolic
visit resonated with me. I'll always remember this
visit and his words because it marked the first time
I returned to the country of my birth. Pope Francis
led with a spirit of reconciliation and encounter, and
for me, the theme of encounter was in everything
I experienced, from meeting family to visiting the
National Basilica Shrine of the Virgin of Charity of
El Cobre.

Encounter. Isn't that what the Blessed Mother
wants for all her children? To encounter her Son?

Pope Francis's visit also had an element of filial
love that is reflected in the gift he took the Blessed
Mother in El Cobre. The pope is known to bring the
Blessed Mother flowers at the Basilica of St. Mary
Major when he returns to Rome. It is a tender offer-
ing from a son. These words from a recent New
Year's Day homily are not just good advice but an
exhortation:

> Devotion to Mary is not spiritual etiquette; it is a
> requirement of the Christian life. . . . The gift of
> the Mother, the gift of every mother and every
> woman, is most precious for the Church, for she
> too is mother and woman.

If our faith is not to be reduced merely to an idea or a doctrine, all of us need a mother's heart, one which knows how to keep the tender love of God and to feel the heartbeat of all around us.[4]

I was moved to see the fresh flowers that Pope Francis placed on the altar by the statue of the Virgin of Charity when he visited El Cobre. I was moved a second time to see them in a vase the next day when I had the opportunity to visit the shrine after he departed for the United States. But Pope Francis left another gift of flowers, this one a little more enduring, as he brought the virgencita a silver vase filled with porcelain flowers in yellow and white.

These three visits—of a "messenger of truth and hope," a "pilgrim of charity," and a "missionary of mercy"—acknowledged and paid tribute to both the spirit and the suffering of the Cuban people. Our Lady of Charity bound them all together, and even though the visits spanned two decades and three papacies, the constant was the Blessed Mother, who has been present to the Cuban people for more than four hundred years.

When I visited the shrine, I was blessed to see the statue of the virgencita on the altar. Pope Francis had celebrated Mass earlier in the day and then gone to the airport with his retinue of priests and attendants. Upon his return from seeing the pope off, the rector opened the shrine for my family to visit, and we had a brief tour. The highlight of the visit was praying a decade of the Rosary at the altar in front of the statue, led by my uncle, the bishop of

Holguin. We were so close to the statue—so close I could have reached out to touch the golden robes. Instead, I pondered the scene—a miracle—beyond a miracle, as never in my life would I have asked for this experience, so far was it from what I thought possible.

And yet here I was, perhaps being called to be a messenger of truth and hope, definitely a pilgrim of charity, undoubtedly a recipient of mercy. The gifts at the Virgin of Charity's altar—a crown for our queen, a rose for our mother, and a bouquet of flowers from her children, near and far—beckoned me close. I left that day knowing I had to share her story with everyone I met. The story of a mother's love for her children.

Baubles, Tokens, and Gifts for the Blessed Mother

I get it when my non-Catholic friends look at me funny when I tell them about participating in a eucharistic procession or when I make plans to attend a special Mass to open a jubilee year. They're pretty used to seeing the tangled rosary I pull out of my pocket as I look for my car keys, the gold medal of Our Lady of Charity that I wear every day, plus a bracelet with a Miraculous Medal given to me after my consecration to Jesus through Mary. I'm not like the crazy cat lady of Catholic sacramentals, but I do love my medals and rosaries. And I have holy water in my desk. Oh, and probably a couple of hundred holy cards and third-order relics.

Maybe I *am* a cat lady of Catholic sacramentals.

Anyway, sacramentals are good, and they are good for us. They remind us of our faith, to pray, to be grateful in all things. They help us be better Christians, and even my non-Catholic friends get that. But what about making gifts to the saints? Why is this a practice?

When my children were little, I encouraged them to pick flowers from my garden to take to Mary for the May crowning at our parish. We'd dress up a little more than usual and go to church early to get in line. It was fun. It was sweet. And it was a perfect child-sized lesson to teach them that veneration is about loving the Blessed Virgin Mary.

I didn't realize that they would adopt this small annual act to areas outside the May crowning. Imagine my delight when one afternoon, while waiting for visiting family to finish an errand at a Catholic bookstore that had a statue of Mary out front, I saw my children placing something along the wall in front of the statue. Concerned they were littering, I went to investigate and discovered they were sharing their stickers with Mary. They were sharing something they loved with the Blessed Mother! I walked away humbled by their generous hearts.

I'm sure Mary loved the stickers as much as I treasured the dandelions and thistles my children brought me. In her eyes, those gifts were probably as precious as gold or porcelain. Wanting to shower our patron saints with gifts is, I think, a beautiful part of our veneration as we admire their lives of holiness and endeavor to learn from them and imitate them. As Catholics, we don't worship these images, but they give us a concrete reminder of the saints in heaven, a representation on earth to help us think about these holy people. We leave gifts because as much as we love flowers and stickers, we love these saints who help us grow in our faith more.

I've learned from my children. Whenever I visit the Ermita de la Caridad in Miami, Florida, I take flowers for my heavenly mother.

Prayer

Oh loving Virgin of Charity, thank you for your presence in my life.

I turn to you to share my worries, my grief, my needs. You listen to all my requests for intercession.

Remember that I love you.

Thank you for being a loving mother to me. Amen.

4.

LOVE UNITES US

Celebrating Our Lady of Charity

I saw the Mother of God, unspeakably beautiful. She said to me, "My daughter, what I demand from you is prayer, for the world and especially your country."

—St. Faustina Kowalska

Stepping Out of My Comfort Zone

I used to spend a lot of time in my car. I would take the children to school and hit a long commute from our home into the city for work. Then I'd do the same in reverse. When my youngest graduated from high school, we calculated all the miles I'd driven while they were in school. It was a staggering number. I admit too many miles were spent, or rather misspent, in mild road rage and general annoyance. Once I wrapped my mind around the idea that these trips could be opportunities to grow in my love of

the Lord, just about every little drive into town
became a time to pray.

I wasn't always successful, but I hope I logged
more good miles than bad. I certainly logged a lot of
laps around my rosary as I prayed in the car. I think
I probably talked off my virgencita's ears in those
carpool days.

These trips, these journeys, were opportunities
to share the road and walk with the Lord; they were
as much about the time spent with him as the destination I wanted to reach. Jesus wants us to walk
with him. He wants us to invite him into our lives,
to make him a part of our every day.

Just as I had compartmentalized the Virgin Mary,
especially under the title of Our Lady of Charity, into
a neat little box of *cubanía* (my cultural identity), I
realized that I had also compartmentalized my relationship with the Lord (my faith identity). I could
rattle off the answers to the catechism questions, but
I didn't really live the words.

I had a routine for everything, and while that
routine helped me stay organized in those years of
raising children and teaching a full load of classes,
it also circumscribed my faith. I rarely brought my
faith out into the sun, and I never let it connect the
moments of my day. Instead of living fully in the joy
of life, I was living each hour of the day as if it was
isolated from the other hours. I went from time to
make breakfast to time to be in the car to time to get
dinner ready. I completed all my chores but didn't
see them as acts of love. At the end of the day, I had
completed many tasks, but I always felt drained and

disconnected. Instead of a meaningful procession of activities that brought me to a sense of accomplishment at the end of the day, I had a disjointed collection of small victories.

Of course I was disconnected. Nothing that I did belonged to anything else. Even when I made time for praying the Rosary, I did not integrate that prayer with the rest of my activities. I was giving Jesus and Mary those twenty minutes for the Rosary, but I wasn't with them the other twenty-three hours and forty minutes of my day. I couldn't wrap my mind around the idea that I should "pray without ceasing" (1 Thes 5:17). What does that even mean?

I had to make an effort to grow in my faith, and the opportunity came to me in the unlikeliest of places: Twitter. I had already stopped listening to the angry, mean morning-commute radio shows and was streaming some entertaining Catholic radio programs instead. One of the hosts introduced an idea that grabbed me right away: he suggested that your first tweet of the day be in thanksgiving, and he called it #gratefultweet. I adopted that idea immediately and continue the practice today. The last time I saw one of his tweets, it was numbered in the thousands, so we've been at this for some years. It sounds a little silly to say this was transformative, but it's true. That small act in the mornings became a prayer. I didn't stop at only one tweet—if something struck me later in the day, I tweeted with the hashtag then, too. Look at that—I had started, with baby steps, to pray without ceasing!

The exhortation in 1 Thessalonians 5:16–18 doesn't mean we are to be praying without stopping in a literal sense but, rather, that we pray throughout our day, making the Lord present to us in each moment. This kind of prayer opens those compartments we create and invites the Lord into our day, maybe even all day. If I tweet about a pretty flower, the next thought is in thanksgiving for it. If I'm in traffic and feel irritation rising, I might pray, "Jesus, I trust in you." I trust that I will get where I'm going. I trust that I am loved even though I feel a little unlovable in my grumpy state. These little aspirations throughout the day are prayer!

In this small way, I came to realize that each day is a pilgrimage as I try to get to where I want to be someday: heaven.

My beloved virgencita mothered me through this growth spurt and helped me walk these little daily pilgrimages. By now, I had holy cards with her image on them scattered about on my desk and in use as bookmarks. I placed a small statue of Our Lady of Charity in a visible place in my home, and I even had a medal that I wore close to my heart. Every glimpse of Cachita was a reminder to say a little prayer, even if it was only, "Jesus, I trust in you." Even if, especially if, the only thing I said was a loving, "Jesus. Jesus."

Opening My Heart to Pilgrimage Set Me on Adventures (and More Pilgrimages)

I still hope to one day embark on a big religious pilgrimage, if not to Jerusalem or Rome then maybe to

Compostela to walk the Camino de Santiago. The idea of a walking pilgrimage appeals to me because of so many years teaching literature, specifically *The Canterbury Tales*, which takes place as pilgrims travel from London to Canterbury Cathedral to venerate the relics of St. Thomas Becket. Recently, my husband and I were in London and took a day trip to Canterbury, so I did make my small walking pilgrimage! It became a spiritual journey for me that awakened a yearning for the Real Presence in the Blessed Sacrament.

Walking through the enormous cathedral while contemplating its history made me profoundly sad. When Henry VIII quarreled with the pope and formed the Church of England, this beautiful cathedral that had once been Roman Catholic became the seat of the Church of England. St. Thomas Becket's shrine was destroyed, and the Blessed Sacrament was removed to make way for the Protestant tradition. As my husband and I walked down the street toward the center of town for lunch, I shared my yearning for the Blessed Sacrament, and we talked about how we had encountered so many desanctified and forgotten Catholic churches on this trip and how I was missing the Blessed Mother, too. I had no sooner said that I wished I could have sat with Jesus for a little while when we discovered a Catholic church down an alley. It was called St. Thomas of Canterbury, and when we entered, we came upon the exposition of the Blessed Sacrament! Is God good, or what? I actually did make a pilgrimage, like the pilgrims in the *Tales,* as St. Thomas Becket's relics are in this church named for the martyr.

Another time a dear friend of mine took me to the Shrine of the Divine Mercy in Stockbridge, Massachusetts. We prayed the Stations of the Cross in the rain, and I remember thinking that a little holy water from heaven was lovely. God doesn't do small, so we didn't get a sprinkling; it was a good soaking rain.

By then, though, I had developed a heart for turning these small trips into pilgrimages by inviting the Blessed Mother and Jesus along on the journey and, whenever possible, arranging a visit to a place of some religious significance to make Jesus and Mary part of the destination, too!

I yearned to make a pilgrimage to Cuba and to the National Basilica Shrine of Our Lady of Charity of El Cobre. That's a big name for a shrine that houses a little statue, isn't it? I kept that desire so closely guarded in my heart that very few people knew about it. It seemed impossible for me, so I let it just sit there. When my sister suggested I go to Cuba for Pope Francis's apostolic visit, that desire fluttered a little, but I still didn't verbalize it. I was already so grateful to be returning to Cuba and so happy to accept whatever graces came my way that I didn't dare ask for one more.

Silly me. I wasn't paying attention to scripture: "Find your delight in the LORD who will give you your heart's desire" (Ps 37:4).

Jesus knew, of course, what was in my heart, and Our Lady of Charity surely wanted me to visit the shrine. I'm certain they put that desire on my heart some years earlier during the activities surrounding the celebration of the four hundredth anniversary of the discovery of the little statue of Our Lady of Charity floating in the Bay of Nipe. The Church in Cuba celebrated this jubilee with prayer, Masses, community celebrations, and a most ambitious plan to reach every corner of the island with a magnificent procession that brought Our Lady of Charity and, most importantly, Jesus Christ, to the people.

I first heard about this jubilee celebration through a request that popped into my inbox one day. A journalist covering the story in both Cuba and Miami was putting together a feature about how far the devotion to Our Lady of Charity had spread. We often think of Cuban immigration after 1960, but the truth is that due to Cuba's proximity to Florida, Cubans have immigrated to the United States in every era. Cachita might be anywhere in the States. I knew there was a statue in Atlanta, Georgia, at the Cathedral of Christ the King. My mission was to get a picture for inclusion in the feature. Easy-peasy. Little did I know it was the first step in a larger pilgrimage to come. I was seeking Mary and didn't realize it until my search had turned into a walk. A walk with Mary that quickly turned into a walk with the Lord.

Caridad nos une—Charity Unites Us

The preparations for the celebration of four hundred years of devotion to Our Lady of Charity of El Cobre were truly a miracle, perhaps even a series of miracles. In 1960s Cuba, Fidel Castro's policies persecuted all religious institutions, particularly the

Catholic Church. Religion of any kind was deemed inconsistent with Marxist–Leninist ideology, and Cuba became an official atheist state. Then, after decades of religious oppression, the Cuban government declared itself a secular state in 1992 following the collapse of the Soviet Union, relaxing but not eliminating its tight squeeze on religious observance.

In 1997 an exception was made to the general prohibition on public religious celebrations. In preparation for Pope John Paul II's apostolic visit to Cuba in January of 1998, Fidel Castro relented to pressure from the Vatican and, as a show of goodwill for the upcoming papal visit, allowed Christmas to be celebrated in public. And what a celebration it was! Castro intended for this to be an isolated incident, but once that door was opened, there was no turning back. The Church in Cuba has publicly celebrated Christmas ever since, and John Paul II's visit would have lasting effects beyond the celebration of the Nativity.

During the papal visit, John Paul II crowned Our Lady of Charity in Santiago de Cuba following an outdoor Mass on January 24, 1998. His homily called to mind occasions in Cuban history when this same statue was taken out of the shrine and Our Lady of Charity was venerated in public processions:

> Beloved brothers and sisters in the faith, never forget the great events connected with your Queen and Mother. With the canopy of his family altar, Céspedes put together the Cuban flag and went to prostrate himself at the feet of Our Lady before beginning the battle for freedom.

The brave Cuban soldiers, the "Mambises," bore on their breast the medal and "medida" of her holy image. The first act of liberated Cuba in 1898 was when the troops of General Calixto García knelt during a solemn Mass at the feet of Our Lady of Charity for the "Mambisa Declaration of Independence of the Cuban People." The various pilgrimages of the image through the towns of the island, heeding the desires and hopes, the joys and sufferings of all her children, have always involved great displays of faith and love.[1]

Although his homily was a reflection on the history of the Cuban people and the veneration of Our Lady of Charity, the pope's words proved prophetic. Fast forward a little more than a decade to August of 2010, when the Conference of Catholic Bishops of Cuba embarked on what was undoubtedly the boldest, most ambitious act of evangelization to occur in Cuba in fifty years: To mark in 2012 the four hundredth anniversary of the discovery of the statue of Our Lady of Charity, the Church began a Marian procession with the statue of Our Lady of Charity of El Cobre encased in protective glass. The procession across the country covered almost twenty thousand miles.

The Catholic Church in Cuba officially embarked on a magnificent pilgrimage, visiting each province in a beautiful procession with the statue of Our Lady of Charity leading the way. Hundreds of thousands of Cubans lined the streets to catch a glimpse of Cachita. Masses were celebrated. Cubans who ordinarily would not have had the means to make a pilgrimage to El Cobre were blessed by the graces that came from this procession.

The theme of this celebration—*A Jesús por María: Caridad nos une*, which means "To Jesus through Mary: Charity Unites Us"—was a powerful statement for the Cuban people. As patroness of Cuba and a symbol of the Cuban people, Our Lady of Charity could not have conveyed a more compelling theme of unity as the statue processed from town to town, province through province, visiting the far reaches of the island nation.

Taking the familiar and beloved virgencita on the road to pay her children a visit in their communities and homes reminds me of another visit, when the pregnant Mary, in the process of visiting Elizabeth, took Jesus to her cousin's home. Mary was the first evangelist then and, now in our time, continues to deliver this message of love. For many who knew Our Lady of Charity as patroness of Cuba and an iconic symbol, this opportunity for catechesis and introducing Jesus Christ to the crowds was the continuation of Mary's message of evangelization.

Four hundred years earlier, the message of Our Lady of Charity made its way across the country by word of mouth, on foot, and on horseback. Today, the procession was led by a van carrying the statue of the Blessed Mother. The procession departed from the shrine in El Cobre and returned almost two years later after wending and winding through Cuba's hills, valleys, plains, and coastline—touching the hearts of her children. The route included stops that were intimate and deeply moving, such as visits to jails and nursing homes, along with the expected visits to churches. No one was excluded—the theme that charity unites conveys the powerful message that we are all Mary's children and she is our mother. There was no distinction for rich or poor, privileged or marginalized. With Mary as their mother, the Cuban people could see themselves as brothers and sisters united by love.

I'm sure that the people touched by this procession still talk about it, and perhaps these areas have seen an increased desire to learn more about Jesus Christ and the Catholic faith. Cachita, I'm sure, was at the very heart of it, carrying her Son in her arms for all to see. It was truly a powerful opportunity for evangelization.

Communism, atheism, and oppression may have tamped down religion, but Our Lady of Charity had remained a visible and active presence throughout Cuba in spite of the years of state-enforced silence. The government may have closed the doors of the churches, but it could not eradicate the popular devotion that was so deeply ingrained in the Cuban people. The procession brought their beloved Cachita out into the streets for people to see. Our Lady of Charity was openly venerated everywhere the procession went and, in doing so, returned Christ to the public square in Cuba.

Love Unites Us

The story of this celebration, however, gets bigger and better. The message "Charity unites us" united all the Cubans across the provinces in Cuba and beyond during that celebratory pilgrimage.

That homily Pope John Paul II delivered in Santiago on January 24, 1998, no doubt the catalyst for this jubilee procession, also spoke of healing. The pope lovingly addressed Cubans who were not in Cuba, alluding to the diaspora that began in 1959 and continues today. There are more than 1.5 million Cubans in the United States alone and unknown numbers throughout the rest of the world. Pope John Paul II spoke to us, too: "From this place I wish to send my greetings also to all of Cuba's children who, in whatever part of the world, venerate Our Lady of Charity; together with all your brothers and sisters who live in this fair land, I place you under her maternal protection, asking her, loving Mother of all, to unite her children once more through reconciliation and brotherhood."[2]

For Cuban Americans of my generation, whose parents have felt the pain of exile from their beloved homeland and whose children are unequivocally American in their speech and mindset but still embrace their cultural connection to Cuba, those words brought tears to our eyes. My heart broke open in that moment. I didn't realize it had been clenched my whole life, not from fear—or worse, some deep-seated hatred or resentment—but because I had been holding my breath in a strange exile-induced limbo that was relieved in that prayer. My generation, as with generations in so many waves of immigration, became the sandwich generation, belonging to neither the old world nor the new one. We lived in both and belonged fully to neither. Pope John Paul II's words validated my belonging to Cuba and belonging to Our Lady of Charity as her child. That homily was, among other things, the seed for the pilgrimage I would one day take to my birthplace at my mother's house in Santa Clara and the shrine in El Cobre, where my heavenly mother is venerated.

Pope John Paul II's words were indeed prophetic. In 2012, the jubilee celebrating Our Lady of Charity crossed the tumultuous waters of the Straits of Florida to celebrate in Miami, too! The year before, in 2011, as the Cuban people were observing the procession of Our Lady of Charity across their nation, there were celebrations in Miami to mark the golden jubilee, fifty years since a replica of the statue was smuggled out of Cuba and sent to Miami to console and inspire hope in the community of Cuban exiles. On September 8, 1961, the Feast of the Nativity of the Blessed Mother and the Feast of Our Lady of Charity, the archdiocese of Miami had celebrated the first Mass for the Cuban exiles, and it has celebrated this feast day every subsequent year. That statue of Our Lady of Charity was kept at St. John Bosco Catholic Church in the Little Havana neighborhood of Miami until construction of the Ermita de la Caridad shrine began in 1967. How providential that this jubilee would fall within the window of celebrations in Cuba!

The following year, in 2012, the archdiocese of Miami once again celebrated Mass, this time for thirty thousand faithful gathered in an arena in Miami to celebrate the four hundredth anniversary of the finding of this little statue and the veneration of Our Lady of Charity of El Cobre. The Mass was celebrated in solidarity with the Church in Cuba. As part of this message of unity, during the jubilee year celebrating Our Lady of Charity, bishops from Cuba went to Miami to celebrate Mass at the Ermita de la Caridad shrine, and Archbishop Thomas Wenski of Miami went to Cuba for the same, both beautiful gestures of unity.

The message was clear: Our Lady of Charity is our mother, regardless of where we might find ourselves in this world. In our true home, we are all brothers and sisters united by the one who is Love. Caridad, as Pope John Paul II prayed, is a vibrant sign of this love:

> Our Lady of Charity of El Cobre, Patroness of
>   Cuba!
> Hail Mary, full of grace!
> You are the beloved Daughter of the Father,
> the Mother of Christ, our God,
> the living Temple of the Holy Spirit.
> Your name, O Virgin of Charity,
> evokes thoughts of the God who is Love.[3]

Taking Love to the World

My earliest memory of participating in a procession was when I was in second grade. All the children who had made their first Holy Communion that spring got to lead the May procession to crown the Blessed Virgin Mary with flowers. Each of us carried flowers from home. The line started quite orderly, but those of us in the back pressed forward a little bit, and then a little more, and soon we lost the look of a line and became more of a joyful mob.

Whenever I think of processions, I remember that joy. It's what I see on the faces of so many Cubans lined along the streets of their towns when I view footage of the Marian procession celebrating Our Lady of Charity. In town after town, people took to the street waving signs and flags. Shouting. Praying. Dancing. In short, they were making a joyful noise.

Scenes such as these occur throughout the world where public displays of the faith accompany celebrations of patron saints or holy days. Processions are special because they take what is holy—veneration of a saint, for example, or the Blessed Sacrament on the Feast of Corpus Christi—out of the sacred space of the church and into the world. This movement in some way sanctifies the outside space. It reminds me that when I go out into the world, I am traveling, following the Blessed Mother's example, as a temple of the Holy Spirit wherever I go—that I can, and should, carry Jesus to the ends of the earth or, at the very least, to my work and play.

Unlike pilgrimages, which take the faithful out of their comfortable surroundings to seek God, processions occur in familiar spaces in the community. Because they are public displays of the faith, they are powerful tools for evangelization in addition to being the source of fruits for the participants.

When I lived in Atlanta, Georgia, I participated in the Eucharistic Congress, which is held every year on the Feast of Corpus Christi. Tens of thousands of Catholics gather for this weekend event, and the eucharistic procession is always a highlight for me. To process behind the Blessed Sacrament is solemn and sublime. Some years I've been unable to join the procession because of my participation in other parts of the Congress. Hearing the bells that precede the procession is a powerful call to holiness. Everyone stops what they are doing and drops to their knees. It is magnificent to experience this devotion, this worship, alongside a group of people who share this love for Christ.

I don't often participate in processions, especially large ones. My experience has been limited to very solemn eucharistic processions, which, frankly, are the pinnacle, right? But a part of me longs to recapture that first Marian procession I experienced as a child and take to the streets with joyful song and an outpouring of love as my brothers and sisters did in Cuba for Our Lady of Charity.

Prayer

Beloved Virgin of Charity,

We, your children, come to you, filled with love for you and your Son, our Lord.

Inspire in us a love for our brothers and sisters. We are all so different—help us to see the beauty of our diversity and teach us to love one another as you love us. Amen.

5.

ERMITA DE LA CARIDAD

Miami's Shrine for the World

Let us run to Mary, and, as her little children,
cast ourselves into her arms with a perfect
confidence.

—St. Francis de Sales

We're All Pilgrims

My earliest understanding of pilgrims, like that
of most little kids in this country, involved som-
ber-looking people dressed in dark clothes with
the unfortunate fashion decision to put big buckles
on everything. And I thought they ate a lot of turkey and dressing. I ate a lot of roast pork and black
beans, so I didn't think I had much in common with
them. Our Thanksgiving didn't look like the Norman
Rockwell feast on the cover of the *Saturday Evening
Post*. Still, every Thanksgiving my family made an
effort to eat turkey—never mind that my mother
marinated the turkey with *mojo*, the same garlicky

vinegar-based marinade she used for pork roasts.
We passed on the dressing, though. Black beans and
rice, plantains, yuca, and a little sweet potato soufflé
as a nod to the traditional holiday fare graced our
dinner table.

Even though we didn't get the Thanksgiving
menu right, we got the sentiment spot on. My family had a lot to be thankful for. First, we were finally
united. My father left Cuba in 1962 a little more than
a month after my parents were married in order to
find work and a place to live. He had a visa and
thought it would be easy to claim my mother once he
was working and settled in the country. They didn't
anticipate that my mom would be pregnant with me
and that the Cuban Missile Crisis and subsequent
blockade would shut down any possibility that they
would be reunited soon, if at all. In fact, it took years
for them to be reunited and for me to finally meet
my father.

I don't remember what we ate that first Thanksgiving together in the United States, but I can say
with certainty that my parents adopted this holiday
immediately and with great fervor—even though
my mother never figured out how to make dressing.

In school, I learned about the pilgrims and
how they risked crossing the ocean to settle in an
unknown land in order to escape political oppression and pursue religious freedom. I thought I must
be a pilgrim, too—we crossed an ocean to escape
political oppression and to pursue religious freedom!
I shared this revelation with my teacher, who kindly

corrected me and explained that we weren't pilgrims but political exiles.

I didn't know what she meant, and neither of us made any more to-do about it. I just kept on thinking we were pilgrims and never mentioned it again.

By the time I was a teenager, I understood the meaning of exile. My parents and grandparents used the word *exiliados* to describe themselves collectively as an immigrant group. They were exiled from their homeland, banished, driven out, rejected as incompatible with the ideology in power.

In those early years of the Communist regime in Cuba, the Cubans in Miami and other pockets of heavy Cuban migration really were in exile, waiting for the opportunity for the political scene in Cuba to sort itself out so they could return to their homes. The years turned into decades, and several generations have come and gone waiting for freedom to return to Cuba.

I have often felt the heavy load of exile. I straddle the shark-infested Florida Straits, one foot firmly in the United States and the other foot slipping and dragging but managing a precarious hold on Cuba. I am neither here nor there. But divine providence has brought me here.

I *was* a pilgrim.

I *am* a pilgrim.

A Pastor and His Sheep

Something happens when you grow up with the brokenness of exile looming all around you: you never feel like you belong. Creating a sense of community becomes an essential step toward healing. Churches, especially, become safe harbors for the drifting faithful. And finding common ground in the familiar can be a balm for this feeling of isolation.

Fr. Agustin Román, a Cuban priest also experiencing the pangs of exile in Miami, immediately dedicated himself to serving these Cuban exiles and became a balm for the community. He was expelled from Cuba in 1961, part of the blow to the Catholic faithful when more than 130 priests and religious were rounded up and forced onto an already full Spanish freighter and passenger ship named the *Covadonga*. Because the ship was full, the priests were forced into the ship's cargo area, where they stayed for the weeklong journey to Spain.

Arriving in Spain with no identification, no spare clothes, no money, and no sense of what the future would bring, Fr. Román accepted an assignment to Chile, where he served until he went to Miami in 1966. When he arrived in Miami, Fr. Román began ministering to the growing Cuban population and explored the possibility of building a shrine to Our Lady of Charity of El Cobre as a monument to the struggles and suffering of an exiled community that loves liberty, loves Cuba, and, most of all, loves the Lord and the Blessed Virgin Mary. Our Lady of Charity, the patroness of Cuba, encompasses all these values. To her the Cuban exiles would anchor their hope for a free Cuba.

With the support of Miami's archbishop, Coleman F. Carroll, Fr. Román, later known to his Hispanic flock as Msgr. Román as a sign of their respect, began the difficult work of building a shrine. The idea was immediately embraced by the exiled Cubans, who were now united by a common cause. The Confraternity of Our Lady of Charity was established to educate, catechize, and provide support for the community.

Within a year, a chapel was built, and Masses were celebrated there. The construction of the shrine was underwritten not by a wealthy benefactor but by the humble offerings of faithful Cubans who gave, like the widow's mite, from their own need. I remember my parents marveling that the shrine was built not with dollars but with pennies given with love.

The National Shrine of Our Lady of Charity, the Ermita de la Caridad, was dedicated on December 2, 1973. It stands mere yards from Biscayne Bay, facing south toward Cuba. The building is shaped like a cone, representative of the Blessed Mother's mantle. The sanctuary and church are in the front, and a small chapel for perpetual adoration is behind the altar. The monstrance holding the Blessed Sacrament, in a glass case in the middle of the chapel, is placed in such a way that it is framed by a stained-glass mural depicting Our Lady of Charity above ocean waves.

I've spent a great deal of time in that adoration chapel. Of course, I am there for Jesus, but the stained-glass mural has a unique draw for me. On sunny days when the bay has a lot of wave action, the reflection of the waves on the stained glass makes the glass waves come to life and move under the image of Our Lady of Charity. It makes me think of how the Blessed Mother moves among her children, gently carrying them in the current.

The sanctuary also has a great deal of sentimental and symbolic emphasis. A huge mural depicting key scenes in Cuba's history shows the presence of Our Lady of Charity throughout the formation of the nation. It's stunning to note that while the Blessed Mother dominates the mural, it is her Son, Jesus Christ, who is fixed exactly at its center.

Immediately below the mural is a replica of the statue that is above the altar at the Basilica Shrine in El Cobre, Cuba. The replica was made in Cuba and smuggled out of the country and brought to Miami in 1961. This statue, like the many Cubans who come to the shrine, is in exile, too. At the foot of the altar is a brick made from dirt and soil from the six original provinces of Cuba and mixed with water from a jug found on a raft where fifteen Cuban refugees perished under the dangerous conditions at sea. The pathos of these symbols is overshadowed by the faith, hope, and charity depicted above them in the mural.

The shrine immediately became a focal point for the many Cubans who were coming to Miami by any means available. Here, under the safety of Mary's mantle as symbolized in the conical design of the shrine, Cachita receives all her children, whether they come in celebration or supplication. Msgr. Román received them all with love and compassion, too.

Msgr. Román served the community in the archdiocese of Miami for decades. He was beloved by many. His accomplishments as priest and auxiliary bishop show his dedication to the dignity of all persons through his work in pastoral service. Sensitive as he was to the trials immigrants faced, he also worked with the growing numbers of immigrants from Haiti, migrant workers, and refugees of all nationalities. Marginalized groups found a good shepherd in Msgr. Román. Thousands of faithful who made pilgrimages to the Ermita were met with the same tenderness and attention as the locals who made a regular habit of attending daily Mass or confessions at the shrine.

The Ermita de la Caridad Is for All Mary's Children

The Shrine of Our Lady of Charity is as much about identity as anything else. Cuban identity and Catholic identity are one and the same for the people who visit the shrine for Mass and to pay their respects to the Blessed Mother, but not all are Catholic or Cuban. The shrine is an active sanctuary for the pilgrim seeking a peaceful place to lay down his or her burdens in prayer or to offer thanksgiving. Many bring offerings of flowers, yellow roses or bright golden sunflowers. A multitude of bouquets adorn the wall just outside the adoration chapel, sometimes so many that they pose a problem for disposal.

When I visit Miami, I often bring flowers to the Blessed Mother in thanksgiving and leave them in the pretty and practical trough designed to hold these gifts. I usually place them there and move into the adoration chapel for a little while before going on with my day. One morning, after placing my flowers among dozens already there, I joined the growing crowd for daily Mass. It was a treat to have timed my visit for Mass. At the end, Msgr. Román blessed the flowers and thanked the faithful for the offering. Then he instructed us to pick up the blessed flowers and take them to someone who needed the loving touch of the Blessed Mother on this day. He asked us to think of the shut-ins, the forgotten, those who needed to be evangelized, and take them these flowers from Mary's own garden. It was a beautiful way to live the love of Our Lady of Charity, and it was a typical display of tenderness from this much beloved servant-leader.

This small gesture had a big impact on me. It was good to honor the Blessed Mother with the gift of flowers and my visit. It was inspiring to be her envoy and carry those flowers to someone who would be blessed by my visit and attentions. What a powerful lesson I learned that day. The gift of flowers was just the catalyst for the real gift, my presence in the life of someone who needed a friend that day. I can reflect on the times others have been an envoy of this love for me.

Msgr. Román's legacy is love. Throughout his decades of service in the Miami community, which included his appointment as an auxiliary bishop to the archdiocese of Miami, Msgr. Román showed his fatherly (and eventually, grandfatherly) love for the Cubans and Cuban Americans who visited the shrine. He served as director of the shrine from the time it was conceived in 1966 until his retirement in 2003 and then remained as rector emeritus until his death in 2012. He died as he lived, under the maternal mantle of Our Lady of Charity of El Cobre. Today, Bishop Román is remembered for his love of Our Lady of Charity, his devotion to the Cuban people, his yearning for a free Cuba, and his love of the Lord, to whom he dedicated his whole life in the priesthood.

Catholics and non-Catholics alike mourned his passing, and his funeral was attended by thousands. His funeral Mass was concelebrated by his brother bishops from Miami as well as two visiting bishops from his beloved Cuba, representing the dioceses of Holguin, where Our Lady of Charity first appeared, and Santiago de Cuba, home of the National Basilica Shrine of Our Lady of Charity of El Cobre.

Today the Ermita de la Caridad draws pilgrims from all over Latin America, continuing to be a refuge for those seeking relief from isolation, oppression, and exile. Sadly, the same Communist ideology that forced Msgr. Román into exile half a century ago and led to hundreds of thousands of Cubans fleeing their homeland has infected other places in Latin America. Some pilgrims come seeking refuge from poverty or violence. Our Lady of Charity calls those children to her, providing succor and relief from the pangs of separation. She offers consolation, and while beholding her image painted on the mural above the altar, we see in her arms the source of love and salvation for all, Jesus Christ.

Seeking God in Pilgrimage

For Cuban immigrants who had settled across the United States in the 1960s and '70s, Miami held a magnetic allure that called them to resettle there. Because the large number of Cubans already in Miami and nearby Hialeah opened businesses that catered to Cuban tastes, my trips there with my family were opportunities to eat lots of Cuban food that wasn't available back home in Atlanta. The corner cafeterias that served Cuban sandwiches, pastries, and coffee around the clock became as little shrines for me. If I saw one, and it was impossible to go a block without spotting one, I wanted to stop for a thimble-sized shot of the sweet coffee.

Growing up in the mid-1970s, I took advantage of these trips to Miami not only to speak Spanish but also to learn Spanglish, the melding of our two languages that was almost synonymous with the melding of our two cultures. Music, too, was an essential part of the pilgrimage. I listened to Led Zeppelin and southern rock at home in Atlanta and was introduced to Celia Cruz in Miami. Gloria Estefan was just starting to sing at local gigs with the Miami Sound Machine.

These trips were definitely a journey into my parents' world and filled a great need I had to belong—to feel a connection with others like me. It helped form my identity.

Part of that identity, of course, was our faith. We attended Mass in Spanish. At the time, it was a novelty for me. We attended Masses in Spanish in Atlanta, but they were often on special occasions.

In Miami, Mass was offered in Spanish on a regular basis at most parishes. It was a matter of choice, but the novelty wore off quickly. I enjoyed making friends with other Cuban American kids, had fun salsa dancing, and could put away a fair share of *croquetas*, little fried balls of breaded ham or codfish—but like my peers, I preferred to speak English and to attend Mass in English.

Too often, the preference didn't matter. We attended Mass with our parents, and if that meant in Spanish, I had better make sure I was on the right page in the missalette.

No trip would be complete without a visit to Our Lady of Charity at her home in Miami—as it's known locally, la Ermita, or simply, "the shrine." It is my first real memory of actively making a pilgrimage. To this day, when I am in Miami, I make time to drop in on my heavenly mother at la Ermita and spend some time in adoration of the Lord in the perpetual adoration chapel. Pilgrims might go to pay their respects to Cachita, but she beckons us to visit her Son as she extends Jesus out to us in the mural above the altar.

La Ermita is one of my favorite places to visit in Miami. More than the beach, more than Calle Ocho and the endless cafeterias offering me delicious morsels of roast pork and black beans. Visiting la Ermita is food and fuel for my spiritual journey. I join thousands and thousands of fellow pilgrims on these visits. Pilgrimages have been a long-standing part of our Catholic faith. They are not essential or required of us, but they do enrich us in many ways.

"Pilgrimages evoke our earthly journey toward heaven and are traditionally very special occasions for renewal in prayer" (CCC, 2691).

Pilgrim sites abound throughout the world. For those who like to travel and have the means, it's certainly a grand experience to visit the Holy Land or Rome. Shrines dedicated to Our Lady of Fatima in Portugal, Our Lady of Lourdes in France, and Our Lady of Guadalupe in Mexico are some iconic pilgrimage sites. Devotion to Our Lady of Akita in Japan is growing. For those who prefer to travel in the United States, we have a rich history here as well. Wisconsin has the only formally approved Marian apparition site in the United States. I hope to visit Green Bay and go to the Shrine of Our Lady of Good Help some day. I've had the pleasure of traveling through some of the mission churches in California, and I've visited other important churches and shrines such as the Basilica of the Assumption in Baltimore, Maryland, the first cathedral in the country. I even grew up in the neighborhood near the Basilica of the Sacred Heart of Jesus in Atlanta, the first basilica in Georgia.

We don't need to travel far to go on a pilgrimage. Our communities often have historic churches or shrines that can serve that purpose. After all, we go on pilgrimage to strengthen our prayer life, to do something out of the ordinary for renewal in our faith. Careful planning and the intention to "be a pilgrim" would probably yield wonderful graces from the experience of a local pilgrimage. But if you're ever in Miami, make la Ermita a special stop on your journey.

When Msgr. Román conceived of building the shrine, he was thinking that Our Lady of Charity would be a consolation to Cuban exiles. There was a time when Our Lady of Charity was only known in Cuba, but today she is recognized throughout the Americas, and knowledge of her continues to spread. Devotion to the Blessed Mother under this title is particularly poignant given the continuing issues the United States is experiencing with immigration. The Holy Family experienced the sorrows and dangers of exile, so appealing to Mary for succor and strength seems a natural response to the hopelessness and despair that spiritually endanger souls when circumstances are overwhelming.

The truth is we are all exiles waiting for the day we are reunited with our Father in heaven. Until then, we are pilgrims here on earth, searching for a place we call home.

In his own lifetime, Msgr. Román must have seen how pilgrims from all over were called to this pretty little shrine on the edge of Biscayne Bay, offering a cool respite from the south Florida heat and, more importantly, a true sanctuary for the aching soul—a place to stop on the journey and be refreshed.

Prayer

Sweet mother, Virgin of Charity, protect all who have recourse to you.

Grant that we always see the Light of your Son on our journey. Should we ever lose sight of him, lead us on the path back to him.

Shower us with the grace to help each other on our pilgrimage on earth.

Pray for us, that we may carry your message of love to all the corners of the earth.

Pray to Jesus for us. Amen.

6.

HOW DEVOTION TO MARY LED ME TO HER SON, JESUS

Never be afraid of loving the Blessed Virgin too much. You can never love her more than Jesus did.

—St. Maximilian Kolbe

Mary Always Points to Jesus

A friend once told me that people with deep Marian devotion are of two types. For some, their love of Jesus Christ opened their eyes to the love of the Blessed Mother. For others, their strong devotion to Mary led them straight to Jesus.

I fell into that second category.

Of course, I loved the Lord when I was growing up. But I also had a very compartmentalized approach to prayer and worship. I attended Mass with my family and understood the eucharistic celebration as our proper worship of the Lord. And then we had extras. There were saints. And there was Mary. I didn't grasp how these parts belonged to the whole. In fact, I carried this lack of understanding well into adulthood. I don't blame anyone for this gap. It just happened.

In my mind, the Blessed Virgin Mary was apart from Jesus. She was a player in the Nativity, and then I didn't pay attention to her in relationship to Jesus again for a long time. I think it took me so many years to complete a consecration to Jesus through Mary because I didn't understand this relationship.

I venerated Mary as the Mother of God and certainly considered her to be a powerful intercessor. I knew her as the greatest of all saints. Certainly, my devotion to Mary as Our Lady of Charity of El Cobre offered me ample opportunities to ponder the Blessed Virgin Mary under many of her titles, with a special affection for her as Cachita, my virgencita.

The problem of seeing Mary in this light was the limitations it imposed. I compartmentalized Mary into whatever my needs were. She is patroness of many things and an intercessor for many more. In my limited faith, I saw the Blessed Mother as merely the provider for my needs and whims, as a small child might look to her mother to help her or care for her. I didn't grow up and out of that mindset for many years. In fact, it took becoming a mother myself to slowly come around to tending to this most beautiful relationship.

First, I had some growing up to do, starting with my relationship with my own mother. I was the needy child who grew into the self-centered teen who matured into a young adult, married, and had children of her own. I slowly shifted from relying completely on my mother to rejecting her advice to embracing her wisdom.

Although my personal relationship with my mother blossomed into a lovely mature friendship, my relationship with the Blessed Mother remained childlike in my young adult years. I needed to grow up in my relationship with Mary, too. I hope Mary accepted my love in all the affectionate diminutives I called her. And I am ever grateful that she waited patiently for me to come around to her as my faith began to mature. Perhaps, one day, I will return to my childlike state and raise my arms to her to be led to her Son.

In the meantime, though, I am relishing my maturing devotion to the Blessed Virgin Mary, and thanks to her, my growing relationship with her Son, Jesus Christ. The more I wanted to get to know Mary as my heavenly mother, the deeper I delved into her humility and the more I saw her in relationship to Jesus. I wanted to understand why Mary quietly pondered all these wondrous experiences instead of shouting out to the whole world. But I don't think Mary was demure to the point of being like a little mouse. One of my favorite scriptural references, the story of the wedding at Cana in the Gospel of John (Jn 2:1–12), shows us a confident and assertive Mary, both as a mother to Jesus and as a disciple. As a mother, she presses her Son for what she knows should be done in the circumstances. As a disciple, she shows us firsthand how to completely put her trust in him. She tells the stewards at the wedding, "Do whatever he tells you" (Jn 2:5).

Mary speaks those words to us, too. Do what he says. Sometimes I need my heavenly mother to repeat those words to me.

I knew the maternal Mary. The image of Our Lady of Charity shows her as a young mother, so it was easy for me, all those years, to think of her as mother and as intercessor. Although I didn't know many more details about Cachita, I knew she was a source of comfort and safety because she saved the Three Juans. Perhaps that was a good start to relating to Mary. If nothing else, I knew I could trust her as I trusted my own mother. But I also knew that wasn't enough. I wanted to know more about Mary as Jesus' disciple. To be honest, this desire started with my commitment to praying the Rosary, and that led to making the decision to consecrate myself to Jesus through Mary.

It was humbling. Both devotions required more from me than I was ready or willing to give. I loved the idea of praying the Rosary, and I loved even more the idea of consecrating myself through this wonderful thirty-day commitment to prayer and contemplation. However, neither fit my lifestyle, and it would take years for me to recognize that these two devotions would never fit my lifestyle. I had wanted a devotion that fit my daily routines instead of changing my daily routines to fit God's will for me. I needed to change.

The Holy Rosary of the Blessed Virgin Mary

I'd like to think that when I pray the Rosary, I am a beatific vision of piety and holiness. Lucky for me,

Mary knows the truth of this. And so does my guardian angel. I'd often heard that our guardian angels complete our unfinished Rosaries. There was a time my guardian angel must have sighed at the sight of my reaching for a rosary. I decided to pick up this devotion at the worst possible time in my life: I was working full time and had children in high school, middle school, and elementary school. My husband was working long hours growing a business. I had a needy dog. If I had a spare twenty minutes in my day, I certainly wasn't going to spend it in prayer.

That is precisely why this was the *best* time to pick up this devotion.

Praying the Rosary, especially with the guides that are available for us online as we learn to maneuver through the prayers and meditations, is fairly simple. The opening prayers are always the same: the Apostles' Creed, the Our Father, three Hail Marys, and the Glory Be. The next part is five rounds of one Our Father and ten Hail Marys, what we call a decade. Each decade has a meditation that corresponds to a "mystery" (a time in Jesus' or Mary's life). These are grouped thematically as the Joyful, Luminous, Sorrowful, and Glorious Mysteries. We place ourselves in the scenes as we pray the Hail Marys as a kind of soundtrack to the scene playing in our minds. At least, that's how I do it.

Does a grocery list or a pressing chore sometimes pop into my mind and interrupt my thoughts? Yes. It used to distress me, but reciting the next Hail Mary on a new bead sets me right again. Like a good mother, Mary gently brings me back into focus on the mysteries, on her Son. The ending prayer is the Hail Holy Queen, and then it gets interesting. I've learned that there are some different or additional prayers depending on when and where you learned the Rosary. Again, this is as simple as using a prayer card until you learn the prayers. My favorite part here is adding all the special devotions, such as asking for prayers from particular saints or even a small litany of the titles of Mary. I live in the archdiocese of Mobile, Alabama, and our cathedral is named for the Immaculate Conception, so I always ask Our Lady of the Immaculate Conception to pray for us. You can guess I always ask Our Lady of Charity to pray for us, too!

I've learned to take my time with the Rosary. There's no point in racing through the words. St. Francis de Sales is often credited with suggesting that everyone should pray for half an hour every morning, a full hour if we are really busy. Maybe he said it, maybe he didn't, but this thought sums up a big need in my life. The crazier I am because of my responsibilities and distractions, the more I need the calming effects of prayer. The simple act of picking up a rosary and crossing myself immediately slows me down.

Unfortunately, when I started this devotion, instead of carving out those twenty minutes for prayer in the middle of the day when I most needed a chance to slow down, I picked bedtime.

In addition to failing miserably, I learned a new vocabulary word: soporific. The Rosary calmed me so much that I immediately fell asleep. On a good night I'd make it to the first mystery, but I guarantee I never made it through to the end of the decade. Maybe this has been your experience, too. I know I've laughed about it with friends. I just needed to change my tack and find a better time to pray. Obviously praying the Rosary late at night after I'm cozy in bed is not a good choice for me. I hope Mary never took it personally. I also fell asleep before I found my place in books. I was notorious for sitting down to a movie and nodding off before the first commercial. If the apostles couldn't stay up and pray with Jesus, I felt sure I was doomed.

The lesson I learned here is to know myself and take an honest inventory of how I spend my time (and how much time I waste). I was too exhausted at night to focus on anything, so I had to find another way. First thing in the morning was also problematic. I had to get three kids to school and then get myself to work, usually for an early morning class. My commute was about twenty-five minutes, and I filled that time listening to an edgy morning radio show, the kind that plays pranks on listeners and gossips about Hollywood. I thought my time could be better spent.

Praying the Rosary in the car turned out to be like having a morning call to the Blessed Mother. It was hard at first. If I couldn't remember a full prayer I'd ask my guardian angel to be a bridge for me, but I got better with practice. The good news is that soon I was able to finish a Rosary. Then another. And then another! Eventually, I was comfortably praying a Rosary every day. I still fumbled with some of the ending prayers and sometimes, if I was distracted, found myself reciting the Rosary in Spanglish, but I can say I truly developed a devotion to this prayer. And then something remarkable happened.

As I was growing in my devotion to Mary and this beautiful prayer, I was finding myself drawn deeper and deeper into the mysteries. So much so that I began to pray the scriptural Rosary during quiet time in the afternoon. And then that wasn't enough, and I started reading the daily scripture. Then I subscribed to a daily devotional with the morning and evening prayer.

Maybe Mary and my guardian angel were high-fiving in a corner. I smile to think so. The Blessed Mother led me straight to the gospels.

Not only has the first hour of the day been the best and most consistent time for prayer for me, but I find that when I put it off for later in the day, I feel unbalanced. I am surprised to say that the busier I get, the more time I try to spend in prayer. I don't need a meme to tell me this is grace.

I started with Mary, in my comfortable and comforting devotion to Our Lady of Charity, but that was just the beginning. The Blessed Mother was calling me to more, and trusting her as I had since childhood, I was happy to take her hand and try something new and a little bit daunting.

Total Consecration to Jesus through Mary

My newfound love of the Rosary led me to joining the work of Rosary Army, an apostolate created by Greg and Jennifer Willits, dedicated to making, praying, and giving away all-twine rosaries. They have a lovely website with forums for discussion, all kinds of resources, and the *Rosary Army* podcast that is a lot of fun but also challenges its listeners. I first learned of St. Louis de Montfort's Total Consecration to Jesus through Mary on their podcast.

Consecration is a serious commitment, a total gift of ourselves to the Lord. We endeavor to become holy through this vow to open ourselves completely for the work of grace in our lives. It shouldn't be taken lightly—in fact, I think my difficulty in following through with the consecration was an indication that I wasn't ready.

My yes needed to be a yes—not a maybe, not a yes most of the time. Jesus made this very clear: "Let your 'Yes' mean 'Yes,' and your 'No' mean 'No'" (Mt 5:37). I wanted to give my yes to this total consecration precisely because I was comfortable asking Mary for help in my life: "Consecrating ourselves to Mary means accepting her help to offer ourselves and the whole of mankind to him who is holy, infinitely holy; it means accepting her help—by having recourse to her motherly heart, which beneath the cross was opened to love for every human being, for the whole world—in order to offer the world, the individual human being, mankind as a whole, and all the nations to him who is infinitely holy."[1]

Although we most often say we are making a consecration to Mary, our consecration is, in fact, to the Lord. We go through Mary because we give ourselves over to Mary's guidance to better love her Son, Jesus. St. Louis Marie de Montfort's recommended method for consecration to Jesus through Mary is probably the most well known, and it sounded easy: twelve days of preparation to help disconnect me from worldly things, followed by three weeks of readings and prayers to increase my knowledge of myself, the Blessed Mother, and Jesus Christ. Thirty-three days of readings and prayers. What could be easier than that?

I was feeling quite pleased with myself. That could only mean this challenge was going to be eye-opening for me.

Sometime around day six or seven of the consecration prayers, I put the book aside "for later." Later never came that day or the next. Or the day after that. By then I felt I had missed the window for consecrating on the feast day I had picked, and I put the book on a shelf, where it gathered dust for the next decade.

I admit I felt like a failure, but I think Mary had a plan for me. I wasn't ready for this consecration because I still didn't grasp the fullness of Mary's relationship to Jesus. Remember, I kept Mary apart from Jesus in my prayers. I was still seeing Mary as the epic intercessor (no doubt about that), but I didn't see her, really see her, in her role in salvation history. To be honest, I didn't even know what that meant.

The little statue of Our Lady of Charity that sat high on my dresser greeted me every morning with a smile and reminded me to say my prayers, but I didn't really know Mary! I began my journey in developing a mature relationship with the Blessed

Virgin Mary, first through meditating on the mysteries of the Rosary—which, as St. John Paul II says, is a journey through the gospels—and then reading as much as I could about the Blessed Virgin.

I had to understand, first, what it meant that Mary was the mother of Jesus. I needed to grasp that this didn't just happen to Mary, but that God had a plan for our salvation and that plan included Mary. When Eve allowed herself to be seduced by the evil one's words and fell from grace, God already knew it would be a woman who would cooperate with his plan for our salvation. A woman who would then be a fountain of grace.

> The Virgin Mary, who at the message of the angel received the Word of God in her heart and in her body and gave Life to the world, is acknowledged and honored as being truly the Mother of God and Mother of the Redeemer. Redeemed by reason of the merits of her Son and united to Him by a close and indissoluble tie, she is endowed with the high office and dignity of being the Mother of the Son of God, by which account she is also the beloved daughter of the Father and the temple of the Holy Spirit. (*Lumen Gentium*, 53)

To be honest, my tidy little image of Mary as Mother of God did not fully take into account the complexity of her relationship with God, as daughter of the Father and spouse of the Holy Spirit. I still don't know everything I'd like to know about Mary, but in the ten years following that first attempt at consecration, I came along in my relationship with the Blessed Mother. I came to understand her as a woman fully committed to God. Fully. Consecration finally held the gravitas I was missing.

> Predestined from eternity by that decree of divine providence which determined the incarnation of the Word to be the Mother of God, the Blessed Virgin was on this earth the virgin Mother of the Redeemer, and above all others and in a singular way the generous associate and humble handmaid of the Lord. She conceived, brought forth and nourished Christ. She presented Him to the Father in the temple, and was united with Him by compassion as He died on the Cross. In this singular way she cooperated by her obedience, faith, hope and burning charity in the work of the Saviour in giving back supernatural life to souls. Wherefore she is our mother in the order of grace. (*Lumen Gentium*, 61)

Finally I felt ready to make my consecration. The timing was right for me, and as far as God-incidents go, a new way to make this consecration had just become available to me. As often happens in my faith life, it is the communion of the faithful, friends who are on this journey alongside me, that not only accompany me but sometimes lead me. One of those friends extended an invitation to participate in a small-group consecration based on the book *33 Days to Morning Glory*, by Fr. Michael Gaitley, M.I.C. I said yes immediately. I thought my chances of completing the consecration were stronger if I was working with a group. I was right. This method of consecration was the way to go for me. It wasn't necessarily easy, but the retreat format of the book, the variety of readings from saints I admired (St. Louis de Montfort, of course, but also St. John Paul II, St. Teresa of Calcutta, and St. Maximilian Kolbe), and the support of my sisters in Christ made the experience rich and beautiful. I made my consecration on the Feast of the Annunciation, March 25, 2012.

In much the same way I stumbled through my relationship with my mom, coming out at the end with a mature and lovely friendship, I am well on my way to a deeper friendship with Mary, and that means a deeper friendship with Jesus. To contemplate Mary is to contemplate Jesus because I cannot do one without the other. Mary cannot be kept inside a neat little box, even though I tried. Everything about her is for Jesus. Everything I consider about Mary is in relationship with Jesus. All I have to do is think of my beloved Cachita, and there is Jesus, in her arms. I contemplate Our Lady of Charity, and she shows me my Savior.

I thought making the total consecration would be the culmination of these joyful relationships. I was wrong. Total consecration to Jesus through Mary was like a jumpstart to my faith. It was a booster. For those of you who are gamers, it was the ultimate leveling up. Instead of an end, a graduation, it was an explosion of grace. My life has since become a nonstop adventure for the Lord.

The fruit of my consecration to Jesus through Mary is both astounding and humbling. This is my third book since then. I'm on the road giving retreats and talks. I've gone on pilgrimage to Cuba once,

and I returned to Cuba as a catechist for a weeklong retreat a year later. I quit my job and moved to
another state in order to give my husband his life-
long dream to retire to the Gulf of Mexico. I have no
idea what the Lord has in store for me next, but I'm
in, all in, and I'm not looking back.

The Blessed Virgin Mary Brings Jesus to Us

Mary is the first disciple. She brought the Good
News of salvation to Elizabeth and then the world!
If I'm going to learn all I can about Jesus and how to
be a disciple, what better teacher is there than Mary?
She knew him best.

The *Catechism of the Catholic Church* not only
acknowledges our desire for devotion to the Blessed
Virgin Mary but also recognizes the devotion as an
integral part of the faith.

> *"All generations will call me blessed"*: "The
> Church's devotion to the Blessed Virgin is intrin-
> sic to Christian worship." The Church rightly
> honors "the Blessed Virgin with special devo-
> tion. From the most ancient times the Blessed
> Virgin has been honored with the title of 'Mother
> of God,' to whose protection the faithful fly in
> all their dangers and needs. . . . This very special
> devotion . . . differs essentially from the adora-
> tion which is given to the incarnate Word and
> equally to the Father and the Holy Spirit, and
> greatly fosters this adoration." The liturgical
> feasts dedicated to the Mother of God and Mar-
> ian prayer, such as the rosary, an "epitome of

the whole Gospel," express this devotion to the Virgin Mary. (CCC, 971)

Many saints have had deep devotion to the Blessed Mother, none more beloved in recent times than St. John Paul II and St. Teresa of Calcutta. We know of St. John Paul II's consecration to Mary and his apostolic motto, *Totus Tuus*—totally yours. His contemporary, St. Teresa of Calcutta, taught me and so many others how to pray her emergency novena: nine Memorares, with a tenth in thanksgiving because St. Teresa was so confident the Blessed Mother would grant her favor. (It works! But sometimes the answer is no.)

Saints through the ages have held the Blessed Virgin Mary in high esteem, and rightly so. But what about Cuba? Does Cuba have canonized saints? Saints with not only deep devotion to the Blessed Mother but also devotion to her under the title of Our Lady of Charity? The answer is yes. Well, sort of. St. Anthony Mary Claret, a Spanish bishop, served many years in Cuba. In fact, he was appointed archbishop of Santiago in 1851, at the heart of the growing devotion to Our Lady of Charity!

In 1839, Anthony went to Rome to ask the pope to make him a missionary. During his stay in Rome, he entered the novitiate to become a Jesuit, drawn by the Spiritual Exercises of St. Ignatius. Fr. Claret would not become a Jesuit, but in his time there he was introduced to St. Louis de Montfort's *Treatise on the True Devotion to the Blessed Virgin*. He consecrated himself to the Immaculate Heart of Mary, and the rest of his life was filled with miraculous encounters with the Blessed Mother. Although he served in many posts, he eventually received his heart's desire to become a missionary.

I first heard about St. Anthony Mary quite by accident. On second thought, it was definitely a God-incident some months after I made my consecration. My work schedule changed unexpectedly, and I was able to attend a morning Mass in the middle of the week. It was on the feast of St. Anthony Mary, and my pastor, delighted to see me there, devoted part of his homily to teaching about this saint. After Mass I learned he spoke about the saint specifically for me, thinking I had gone to celebrate the feast day! What a blessing to have learned about a new saint, and truly, what a blessing to have a priest-friend give me that gift.

Years later I recalled what I had learned about St. Anthony Mary Claret when I encountered his portrait in churches in Holguin, Cuba, where he had served so many years ago. I had forgotten all about this amazing man of God and was reminded of him in the very place he had lived. His life was a wonder, but the story that caught my heart connects him, in a dramatic way, to the Three Juans.

As a youth, Anthony had a strong devotion to the Blessed Mother and prayed the Rosary daily in addition to frequently participating in the sacraments. He began preparing for the priesthood as a boy, even taking private Latin lessons. However, his family's circumstances changed, and Anthony went to work as a weaver and demonstrated a great talent for this art. He spent years in Barcelona, Spain, studying new techniques and gave up his vocation to the priesthood.

One hot day, while out on a walk along the shore, he decided to step into the water to cool down. He was wading in the shallow water when a wave came up and carried him out to sea. Terrified because he couldn't swim and overtaken by the large waves, he called out to the Virgin Mary to rescue him, and he was taken back to the safety of the shore. He recognized immediately that this was a sign that he should return to his studies for the priesthood. From that moment on, he endeavored to live his life to honor Mary and serve the Lord. I'd say he was destined for his appointment in Cuba!

St. Anthony Mary Claret's devotion to Mary saved his life when he was a young man, but I'd say the Blessed Mother's intercession in that moment of fear and danger set into motion the events of a lifetime that would not only save his soul but bring others to Mary and Jesus Christ, too. His adventures are stunning, filled with high intrigue, attempts on his life, and reports of crossing vast distances at the blink of an eye. Eyewitnesses attested to the presence of angels helping him travel in his ministry. The most amazing miracle occurred in the presence of the Sisters of Perpetual Adoration, who saw the Blessed Virgin Mary hand St. Anthony Mary the infant Jesus.

Although my life's work as a teacher of composition has been with words, I tend to pray not with words but with images. Often, the scene that comes to my mind is Our Lady of Charity poised to hand Jesus to us. Surely the Blessed Virgin Mary under this title would have been near and dear to St. Anthony Mary during his assignment in Cuba.

The image of Mary handing Jesus to me is one that I pray with often. Perhaps this scenario comes to my mind because of years of seeing images of Our Lady of Charity all around me. She holds a happy Jesus facing me with his arms outstretched, and my maternal sensibilities want to take the infant into the safety of my arms. He's precious. Lovable. Vulnerable.

But is there anything more vulnerable than our Savior hanging on the Cross?

I cannot receive the Babe in Mary's outstretched left arm, the Incarnation of the Word, without also taking the cross of salvation that she holds in her right hand. She brings us love.

• • •

Our Lady of Charity, pray for us.

ℱINAL WORD

Y si vas al Cobre, quiero que me traigas, una virgencita de la caridad.

The chorus to the classic Cuban song "Veneración" implores visitors to the easternmost part of Cuba where the Basilica Shrine of Our Lady of Charity stands high on a hill, to return with a little statue of the virgencita as a souvenir. I had to sing out loud to get the words that open this chapter right on the page—so ingrained are these lyrics in my heart and, I confidently say, in the hearts of my family and many friends.

My identity as a daughter of Mary—my life, with its complications and hyphenations, joys and sorrows—my faith, an exquisite gift of grace—are all inextricably bound to Our Lady of Charity of El Cobre. She is the virgencita who has accompanied me my whole life as she accompanied her Son.

Even when I left her, she never left me. It's impossible to be of Cuban heritage and not constantly encounter Our Lady of Charity in a storefront, at a restaurant, and especially in a home. Cachita popped up in all the places I visited and reminded me that she was present. Reminded me, with Jesus in her arms, that he was with me, too.

Our Lady of Charity of El Cobre watches over all her children even though they are scattered far and wide. It's what a mother does. If there is grace in the suffering of the Cuban people, those who for centuries have lived in periods of oppression, it is because the Blessed Mother is a fountain of grace. If there is grace in the periods of exile experienced by Cubans who have immigrated to other countries in different eras, it is because the Blessed Mother accompanied her children to the ends of the earth. Wherever the Cuban people have gone, they have brought with them their beloved Cachita and, in doing so, have become missionaries of love. Her message of love is unmistakable as she carries Jesus in one arm and a cross, the symbol of his passion, in the other.

This is the story that Cachita tells us—she is Our Lady of Love.

ᴀCKNOWLEDGMENTS

It has not escaped my notice that a book about Our Lady of Charity has been a labor of love. I am grateful for the loving encouragement I received from friends and acquaintances who expressed enthusiasm for this project; for my editor, Amber Elder, who pushed when I needed pushing and cheered when I needed cheering; for Katherine Robinson's vision of the content in a lovely cover; and for the team at Ave Maria Press for taking a manuscript and producing a book. Thanks always to my family for countering my disappearances and moods with love and support, especially for the sacrifices that led to two epic trips to Cuba! And of course, to la virgencita, who has accompanied me throughout my life, showing me the way to her Son.

Notes

1. Mary Rescues Us from the Storm

1. Quoted in Carol Kelly-Gangi, *365 Days with the Saints: A Year of Wisdom from the Saints* (New York: Wellfleet Press, 2015).

2. John Paul II, *Rosarium Virginis Mariae* (*On the Most Holy Rosary*), October 16, 2002, https://w2.vatican.va/content/john-paul-ii/en/apost_letters/2002/documents/hf_jp-ii_apl_20021016_rosarium-virginis-mariae.html.

3. John Paul II, *Rosarium Virginis Mariae.*

2. Mary Embraces the Dignity of Her Children

1. The road from Barajagua to El Cobre was quite busy in those days, as the route was essential to the mining company for trade. It would certainly be an easy route out of El Cobre with a small statue hidden in a pack.

3. Patroness of Cuba

1. John Paul II, "Apostolic Journey of His Holiness John Paul II to Cuba (January 21–26, 1998): Homily," January 24, 1998, https://w2.vatican.va/content/john-paul-ii/en/homilies/1998/documents/hf_jp-ii_hom_19980124_santiago.html.

2. John Paul II, "General Audience of January 28, 1998," https://w2.vatican.va/content/john-paul-ii/en/audiences/1998/documents/hf_jp-ii_aud_28011998.html.

3. John Paul II, "Welcome Ceremony Address of John Paul II," January 21, 1998, http://w2.vatican.va/content/john-paul-ii/en/speeches/1998/january/documents/hf_jp-ii_spe_19980121_lahavana-arrival.html.

4. Hannah Brockhaus, "Pope on New Year's Day: Devotion to Mary Is a Must," Catholic News Agency, January 1, 2018, https://www.catholicnewsagency.com/news/pope-on-new-years-day-devotion-to-mary-is-a-must-10900.

4. Love Unites Us

    1. John Paul II, "Apostolic Journey of His Holiness John Paul II to Cuba (January 21–26, 1998): Homily."

    2. John Paul II, "Apostolic Journey of His Holiness John Paul II to Cuba (January 21–26, 1998): Homily."

    3. John Paul II, "Apostolic Journey of His Holiness John Paul II to Cuba (January 21–26, 1998): Homily."

6. How Devotion to Mary Led Me to Her Son, Jesus

    1. John Paul II, "Mary's Message of Love," May 13, 1982, http://www.ewtn.com/library/PAPALDOC/jp820513.htm.

BIBLIOGRAPHY

Brockhaus, Hannah. "Pope on New Year's Day: Devotion to Mary Is a Must." Catholic News Agency. January 1, 2018. https://www.catholicnewsagency.com/news/pope-on-new-years-day-devotion-to-mary-is-a-must-10900.

Calloway, Donald H. *Under the Mantle: Marian Thoughts from a 21st Century Priest.* Stockbridge, MA: Marian Press, 2013.

"Full Text of Saint Faustina's 'Diary.'" Congregation of the Sisters of Our Lady of Mercy. Accessed July 14, 2018. https://www.faustyna.pl/zmbm/en/diary-full-text.

Guedes, Salvador Larrúa. *Historia de Nuestra Señora La Virgen de la Caridad del Cobre: Reina, madre y patrona de la isla de Cuba.* Miami, FL: Ediciones Universal, 2011.

John Paul II. "Apostolic Journey of His Holiness John Paul II to Cuba (January 21–26, 1988): Homily." January 24, 1998. https://w2.vatican.va/content/john-paul-ii/en/homilies/1998/documents/hf_jp-ii_hom_19980124_santiago.html.

———. "General Audience of January 28, 1998." https://w2.vatican.va/content/john-paul-ii/en/audiences/1998/documents/hf_jp-ii_aud_28011998.html.

———. "Mary's Message of Love." May 13, 1982. http://www.ewtn.com/library/PAPALDOC/jp820513.htm.

———. *Rosarium Virginis Mariae (On the Most Holy Rosary).* October 16, 2002. https://w2.vatican.va/content/john-paul-ii/en/apost_letters/2002/documents/hf_jp-ii_apl_20021016_rosarium-virginis-mariae.html.

Johnston, Francis W. *The Voice of the Saints: Counsels from the Saints to Bring Comfort and Guidance in Daily Living.* Rockford, IL: TAN Books, 1986.

Kelly-Gangi, Carol. *365 Days with the Saints: A Year of Wisdom from the Saints.* New York: Wellfleet Press, 2015.

Montfort, Louis-Marie Grignion de. *True Devotion to the Blessed Virgin.* New York: Montfort Publications, 1975.

Paul VI. *Lumen Gentium.* November 21, 1964. http://www.vatican.va/archive/hist_councils/ii_vatican_council/documents/vat-ii_const_19641121_lumen-gentium_en.html.

Perna, Tom. "10 Quotes about the Blessed Virgin Mary from St. John Vianney." Catholic Exchange. August 26, 2015. https://catholicexchange.com/10-quotes-about-the-blessed-virgin-mary-from-st-john-vianney.

Roth, Daniel Shoer. *Agustín Román: Pastor, profeta, patriarca.* Miami, FL: Ermita de la Caridad, 2015.

Zúñiga, Olga Portuondo. *La Virgen de la Caridad del Cobre: Símbolo de cubanía.* Santiago de Cuba: Editorial Oriente, 1995.

Maria Morera Johnson is the author of the award-winning books *Super Girls and Halos* and *My Badass Book of Saints*. She also contributed to *The Catholic Mom's Prayer Companion, Word by Word: Slowing Down with the Hail Mary,* and *Gaze Upon Jesus.* A CatholicMom.com blogger and educator, Johnson retired in 2016 from her positions as a composition and literature professor and the director of English learning support at Georgia Piedmont Technical College.

Johnson has spoken at a number of events, retreats, and conferences, including the National Council of Catholic Women, Austin Women's Conference, and the Catholic Press Association. She also has been featured on CatholicTV and Busted Halo and in *Catholic Digest* and *St. Anthony Messenger.*

Johnson is a native of Cuba. She and her husband, John, have three grown children and live in the Mobile, Alabama, area.

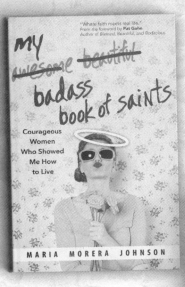